MW01102342

EUREKA!

seven one-act

plays for

secondary schools

selected by

Jacquie Johnston Lewis

and Dianne Warren

COTEAU BOOKS

Edited by Jacquie Johnston Lewis and Dianne Warren.

Cover photographs by Don Hall of Thom Collegiate students. Front cover photograph: Reagan Choboter; back cover photograph (large): Heather Yeo; back cover photograph (small): Susan Cooper and Chad Stewart. Thanks to all the students who took part in the photo shoot.

Cover design by Dik Campbell.

Book design and typeset by Val Jakubowski.

Printed and bound in Canada.

Song lyrics in "Dreamkeeper" are used with the kind permission of Winston Wuttenee ("Kayas Nehiyaw") and The Seventh Fire ("Buffalo Jump").

Thank you to Judy Bear and Mary Jane Eley of the Saskatchewan Indian Federated College for their assistance with the Cree spellings and translations.

The publisher gratefully acknowledges the financial assistance of the Saskatchewan Arts Board, the Canada Council and the Department of Communications.

Canadian Cataloguing in Publication Data

Eureka!

(The Florence James series)
ISBN 1-55050-059-7

1. One-act plays, Canadian (English) - Saskatchewan.*
2. Young adult drama, Canadian (English) -
Saskatchewan* 3. Canadian drama (English) -
Saskatchewan.* 4. Canadian drama (English) - 20th
century.* I. Johnston Lewis, Jacquie, 1950-
II. Warren, Dianne, 1950-   III. Series.

PS8315.5.S2E87 1994   C812'.041089283   C94-920063-8
PR9198.2.S22E87   1994

COTEAU BOOKS
401-2206 Dewney Ave.
Regina, SK S4R 1H3

Contents

Introduction. 1
Jacquie Johnston Lewis and Dianne Warren

Dreamkeeper 3
Bruce Sinclair

> A series of dream sequences in which the characters explore the
> present and future worlds of Aboriginal peoples in Canada.

The Park. 19
Geoffrey Ursell

> A principled individual stands up to the establishment in an
> attempt to preserve a home and the local park.

Me 'n' Alfred 41
Beechy High School Drama Club

> Flashbacks punctuate the life of a homeless man who has lost his
> family and job due to his drinking.

Wheel of Justice. 69
SUNTEP Theatre

> A humorous yet ironic depiction of the trial that Christopher
> Columbus might endure if he were arrested for the "discovery"
> of North America.

Switching Places 95
Rex Deverell

> A look at the difficulties of teenage sex, pregnancy and single
> parenthood – with a twist.

Men and Angels. 129
Lynn Kirk

> The heir to a fortune and a cleaning woman examine the
> possibility of not pursuing one's dreams.

No Means No! 149
Richard Frost, Greg Olson and Lyle Johnson

> A dramatic and emotional account of the effects of date rape on the
> lives of teenagers.

Introduction

Jacquie Johnston Lewis and Dianne Warren

ONE OF THE WONDERFUL THINGS
about involvement in the Arts is the revelation that comes when
events, sounds, words, movements, and images come together in
just the right way and connect with an individual's own knowledge
and experience. Suddenly, there it is ... Eureka! ... a moment of
understanding that one cannot necessarily put into words. A
moment of connection between thoughts and feelings, between
intellect and soul.

When we selected the plays for this anthology, we thought about
these moments of understanding and how they grow from a balance
between accessibility and challenge. Because the plays in this
collection were developed by Saskatchewan playwrights or student
collectives, they offer familiarity through their locales, themes,
language, and characters. However, they also offer challenges:
through their diversity, their sometimes controversial subject matter, the unique perspectives they explore, their staging demands,
and the visions of their creators.

There were many practical considerations in making our selection. We believed it was important to include plays that would be
appropriate both for production and for study in high school drama
and English classes. We looked for variety in cast sizes and staging
so that schools could select plays for production according to their
own students' needs. We looked for themes and styles that offer
ample opportunity for reflection, discussion, and writing activities.
And, finally, we chose plays that we thought would inspire students' own drama creations.

Although it was not our intention to survey the history of plays
and drama in Saskatchewan, we did want to include plays from a

variety of sources. *Dreamkeeper, The Park,* and *Men and Angels* were written by individual playwrights from their own unique perspectives. *Switching Places* was also written by an individual playwright, but because it was written specifically for a theatre company's school tour, it was written in collaboration with other theatre professionals. *Me 'n' Alfred, Wheel of Justice,* and *No Means No!* were developed as collective creations or collaborative efforts. We believe that these seven plays comprise a fair representation of the forty-some plays that were submitted to us.

Finally, there is a celebratory aspect to this collection of plays. Too often students conclude (as a result of what they don't study rather than what they do) that the only worthy play is one written by an English or American playwright, long dead. The plays in this collection were selected with respect for our own time and place, our own issues and dilemmas, and the diversity of experience in our own province. Although we don't believe for a minute that plays written elsewhere and in another time are no longer relevant, we do believe that students in this province will only benefit from seeing their own and each other's lives reflected in the drama they study and perform.

Dreamkeeper

Bruce Sinclair

DREAMKEEPER WAS THE CUL-
mination of a long and exhilarating journey in which I experienced
the many faces of life depicted in the play. Each character is
naturally an extension of myself, some disjointed, some extreme,
and others as honest as possible to my own perception of self. I will
leave it to those who know me to determine which is which. But
the characters, the desperate, volatile man on the street, the
aspiring intellectual and impromptu storyteller, the frantic and
ambitious politician, and the intense, spiritual messenger of the
future, are also a part of all those I have met, to borrow a phrase from
Tennyson.

Each character reflects paths I have travelled, sometimes losing
my way in the maze of concrete and neon, and sometimes becoming
disoriented in the philosophies and aspirations of mankind. In my
life, I have encountered many characters with traits such as these,
some more connected to their roots, others living in the twentieth
century in a state of apathy or complacency.

I write to reflect the world as it is, to escape to a place where I
recognize the need for change, and to create new worlds. But I must
also recognize that we can learn so much from the past if we take the
time to visit that period through literature, stories or our dreams.
Dreamkeeper is set in contemporary times, with the exception of
the last character, the most dreamlike. It is up to you to decide
which is a dream and which is attainable. I sincerely hope that my
dream will be a part of yours and that we can join the spirits with
the knowledge that we can still dream.

For those performing this play there are some things that may
prove helpful to understanding the intent and ultimate message

of the piece. First, a number of swear words have been edited, primarily from the man on the street and the leader of the Eagle Party. It is important to understand that these characters do not respect themselves, and thus, disrespect their language, also. I have substituted other words to satisfy readers who feel that the use of profane words are not necessary. However, I feel very strongly about realism in writing and am sacrificing a part of my artistic integrity in order for students to get a chance to understand the overall intent of the play.

In response to possible questions about who should perform the play, I believe it is certainly a natural vehicle of expression for the original peoples of this continent. I urge others to educate themselves on the term "appropriation." If you are sincere in your expression, that is all that matters, but be sure that you show and ask for respect. I hope that you, as the reader, are aware that the issues raised in *Dreamkeeper* apply to all the human race as well as to my brothers and sisters. We all have suffered, and continue to suffer, from various forms of discrimination, racism, poverty, drug and alcohol addictions, loss of spiritual self, loss of culture, especially language, and oppression from authority. I ask you to look at the Dreamkeeper and find something in his dreams that relate to you. Once you discover this connection, apply it to your world and summon your creativity. It will come in forms and shapes that will amaze you. I will always be grateful to share my story and hope that in some way it will help you express your own beauty and spirit. I pray that we someday find our common family. We are all related.

Bruce Sinclair was raised in the Meadow Lake/Battlefords area of Saskatchewan, and has been involved in theatre since 1986. He has performed with Native Earth Performing Arts in Toronto, in the 1990 production "Diary of a Crazy Boy." He also appeared as The Man in "The Crackwalker" at Persephone Theatre. Bruce is a student in a Métis Teacher Education Program at SUNTEP, University of Saskatchewan, and hosts a radio show, "Red Skies" on CFCR 90.5 FM.

PREMIERE PRODUCTION

Dreamkeeper was produced by Twenty-Fifth Street Theatre Centre in Saskatoon, Saskatchewan, November 8 - 16, 1991. It was directed by Tom Bentley-Fisher. The cast was:

MAN .... Bruce Sinclair
SINGER .... Cheryl Ogram

CHARACTERS

MAN: *Each scene can be played by a different male*
SINGER: *Female with a guitar*

SET DESCRIPTION

The stage is plain. Stage right, a SaskTel telephone booth sits lonely. At centre stage, down, is a wooden stool where the singer sits throughout the play until the end. Stage left is a round table with a leather executive chair, both on a raised platform. A stylistic eagle backdrop is suspended behind the table and chairs.

Scene One

Two spotlights come up simultaneously, one on a woman holding an acoustic guitar sitting on the stool, back centre stage, the other on a man sitting front row centre in the audience. He is deep in sleep with his head down, with one leg resting on the other. The singer begins to strum notes on her guitar, a beautiful song, the introduction to "Kayās Nehiyaw." As the chords wash over the audience, the man slowly, almost imperceptively, begins to wake up. Slowly and powerfully, the notes of the guitar are heard and the beginnings of a Cree chant emanate from the woman. The man, at last, is pulled completely from his sleep and he rises, drawn toward the sound and the dream. He stands and moves forward as in a trance, searching for the source of this sound. Both lights go down slowly. As the chords fade from the woman, the song "Buffalo Jump" by The Seventh Fire comes up and continues into the next scene.

Scene Two

Spotlight comes up on Indian man dancing animatedly to "Buffalo Jump." He is dressed in a jean jacket with an Indian chief embroidered on the back. Around his head are headphones repaired with tape, connected to a Walkman fastened to his belt. In need of a shine, downtown boots and outdated designer tight jeans complete the ensemble. His hair is long and unkempt, held in place by a red bandanna with designs on it. He stalks the telephone booth, keeping the beat of the song with his hips. On the telephone booth is crudely painted with red paint "Oka Warrier." (Purposely misspelled.) He checks the coin return slot on the telephone. Song ends and he tears the headphones off.

MAN: *(laughs)* Oh wee, that's a mighty fine song.... Man, you should have seen me down at Tommy Gunn's last night ... I was cooking ... I mean, you couldn't even touch me, I was soaking wet.... Hot daddy ... oh wow ... I almost forgot man *(pulls beer can from inside jacket)* Damn, she's almost history ... mmmm ... that tastes gooood.... *(spots pedestrian walking by)* Hey buddy, ya got a smoke? *(no response)* Hey, can I bum a smoke?? Hey up yours, you.... Cheap bastard... he probably has a carton in his sock.... You know, man, people aren't the same anymore... tight or whaaat!! *(pauses, senses hopelessness)* Well... what are ya gonna do? *(pulls out harmonica, attempts an imitation of a Chicago bluesman)* Wallll, I ain't got nobuddy, I aiiiin't got nobody, I sez I ain't got nobody to loooove *(wails away for a few seconds, then stops)*... man, this is borrring... I wish it would hurry up and get dark so I can make some cash, this sucks... I wish I had a quarter for the phone *(spots another pedestrian)*... hey bud... hey... yeah you, c'mere... hey, ya got a loonie I could borrow for a couple secs... no... well, hey how about a quarter for the phone... yeah... hey, thanks... I'll pay you back when I get my GST... Ha, ha... yeah right, you stupid son of a... take a hike eh.... *(inserts quarter in the phone)* Hey... Jimmy, how you doing... Where's Mommy?... get Mommy okay?... Look, Jimmy, I'll talk to you later, get your mom... it's important.... *(pause)* Jeez, I hate it when kids answer the phone.... Hey June... how's it going? How's the kids and Marty? Good. Good. Yeah, I was just hanging out and I thought I'd give you a call and see how you're doing? Yeah.... Me? I'm not working right now, no.... Aw... sis... don't be like that ... you know what it's like in this stupid ass town, there's never any work in construction. Jack says he's gonna drive up to Lloyd and try and get on the upgrader, you know, and he said I could go too, y'know, if I chipped in for gas and that... yeah... well, it's worth a shot anyways... say, listen up sis, how's the cash situation? Do you think you could lend me forty bucks? I've gotta get a few supplies, y'know... milk and bread and stuff... really? Oh no, well, when do you think you'll get a cheque??? Two weeks!! Great. I'll be dead by then... I'm just kidding, sis, take it easy, hey... yeah, what?... Oh... they won't give me dick. I don't know why.... What'd they say?? Oh yeah, I have no permanent address or something.... Yeah, well, I'm staying at Julie's but I think she's fixing to give me the boot... yeah, it's basically over, I think.... What?? You seen her??? When??? *(long pause)* Look sis, I gotta go... I'll call you and let you know what happens in Lloyd, okay? Yeah

… I love you too.… *(angrily)* Look!! I can take care of myself. Bye. *(hangs up phone abruptly, searches in breast pocket, finds a marijuana roach, straightens it out and lights it up, coughs a series of sick coughs after inhaling, finishes off beer in can and throws it violently, pulls out harmonica again, begins to sing)* .… No cash, no bread, no sōniyās.… Well, I ain't got nobody … I ain't got nobody, I said.… I ain't got … nobody … to loooove.… Hey, what the hell are you staring at? *(to audience)* Okay, so I hit her, so what?? And you know what? … I'd probably do it again.… Well, what would you do? Man … every night it's the same old thing … were you looking for a job? … we need milk … we need smokes … we need pampers.… I just couldn't take it anymore!!! … Serves her right.… She told me to go see a counsellor.… You know what I told her? I said go to hell! I mean, what's some white dude in some office gonna tell me about hitting my woman? … *(long pause)* I tried, man … I took a course in forestry.… Did real good too, y'know, I had a seventy per cent average.… Man, I don't know how many nights I stayed up studying, drinking tea and smoking cigarettes.… You know where it got me? Nowhere, man, zero. You wanna know where all my buddies are now from class? They're on welfare, man or they're in the joint. Losers. They're stupid, man. They got caught. Well, not this dude.… Noooo way … I know where I can get money.… Don't need nobody … nosirreee. I think I'll go git me some right now.… *(pauses, sniffs the air)* .… Hey, I smell bannock.

Exits. Lights down.

SCENE THREE

From offstage, we hear the sound of Métis fiddling. It is the one and only Hap Boyer, renowned over the entire province, and the sound of his composition, "Rabbit Stew Jig."

MAN *enters jigging and carrying a ghetto blaster with Hap's tune blaring out but not loud enough to drown out his voice, which is also loud but not overpowering. He is wearing beaded mukluks, a Métis sash (red), and a white dress shirt. His hair is in a ponytail. He jigs past the woman onstage, curtsies to her and, seeing the audience, jigs in a lazy clockwise circle toward the first row of seats. He sets the ghetto blaster on a stool that he has pulled out from the front row centre seat the dreamer had vacated, continues jigging, and simultaneously delivers his lecture. The lights have followed him from his entrance past the woman to an area upstage centre. He begins his lecture when he "spots" the audience for the first time.*

MAN: Good afternoon, class. What you are witnessing here is a dazzling exhibition of Métis jigging, possibly not the most professional exhibition, but nevertheless, a reasonable facsimile thereof. Now Métis jigging is a combination of dance styles, the Indian powwow steps, and the Irish and/or Scottish reel, originating in the Red River area with the arrival of the first Europeans to Rupert's Land and making its way through the West with the Métis in the seventeenth century, where it is now enjoying tremendous popularity, particularly in the Western provinces of Manitoba, Alberta, and Saskatchewan. Welcome class, to Native Studies One Oh whatever, the history of the Métis in Canada. *(song ends, he hits stop button on the ghetto blaster, attempts to compose himself, smiles, breathing hard, and gazes at his "class" as if trying to figure them out)* Okay... let's see who we got here... alright.... How many of you are Indians???? How many of you are Métis? *(looks at vacant chair where the dreamer was sitting)* How many of you are sleeping?? Reasons for pointed questions... I have learned through experience that there are a great number of people completely ignorant of the history of the Métis, and for that matter, the Indian in this territory, despite the fact that we live in one of the most heavily populated areas of Aboriginal people in the world.... *(looks at empty chair)* Excuse me ... but could you wake up your buddy there? Thank you.... As you can see from glancing at your class outline, we are going to focus on the Métis from a different perspective than in previous courses, that is... a Métis perspective... we will look at the Métis in the Riel Rebellion through Métis accounts, and continue to discuss and analyse such diverse terms as *(delivered in rapidfire sequence)* assimilation, appropriation, cultural deprivation, degradation, ethnocentricity, is it a word folks? ... recidivism, recognisance, recalcitrant, and lots and lots of other excrement... *(pause, glances at empty seat)* Hello... Hello.... *(pulls out bumper sticker)* Could I interest you in a Métis bumper sticker?? *(slows down, visibly relaxes, and begins speaking in a different tone of voice)* I'm going to tell our friend a little bedtime story. *(lights dim, sits on stool directly opposite from the empty seat)* A long long time ago there was this little Métis boy who lived on the plains with his grandmother.... All this little boy had was his grandmother and every night about twilight, the little boy would snuggle into his Kōkum's arms and she would tell him stories in Michif about the days of the buffalo hunters.... She took that little boy to a world that was long gone... a world where men and women and children lived and died on these prairies... where horses, buffalo, dances, feasts, fiddle playing, and laughter filled the air. She spoke of tall dark men who charged across the high grass in their beautiful beaded fringed jackets.... Métis sashes blowing in the wind.... She spoke of terrible battles where men shot and stabbed each other for things the little boy could not understand.... She told of Indians... warriors and powwows. She spoke of the Cree and the Saulteaux and the Irish and the French and the Scots.... She talked about crying and pain and hunger... until finally, the little boy's eyes would get heavy and he would fall asleep and dream of these stories and wish that he, too, could ride across the prairie with the buffalo hunters.... This is where I would like to take you... to a place that is not in your history books. I want you to try my moccasins and come with me on a journey where you will learn and appreciate another way of life... a way of life where people were willing to die for what they believed in ... a place where men like Louis Riel and Gabriel Dumont were not the exception, but the rule... a time to meet real people with heart, flesh, and blood and bone... that laugh and cry just like you.... *(gets up slowly from stool and whispers)* If you could do me one favour before you leave and that is to please leave very quietly so we don't wake up our friend... perhaps he too is dreaming of riding with the buffalo ... *(stops, sniffs air)* Psst... anybody here smell bannock??

Exits. Lights down.

SCENE FOUR

Spotlight up on the woman. She begins to sing the first two verses of the original song "Sad Man." As song fades, lights up on man entering, talking on cellular phone. He is wearing a black suit jacket and black oxfords. He enters stage left and goes to the small round table and the executive leather swivel chair. Behind the table and chair, suspended from the ceiling, is a backdrop of a stylized eagle on an off-white background. The eagle is black and blue with red eyes.

MAN: Okay, okay... so what do you think we should do? *(to imaginary crew)* C'mon... I ain't got all day... *(to phone)* You're the expert... do you really think that uranium's gonna do it?... I mean, think about it, Jack... if those save the earth crazies get to the premier, you might as well stick a fork in us... we'll be done... well done.... Yeah, yeah, I know, I know!! Listen up, I'm gonna think about it for awhile ... call me back... right *(hangs up phone)*... okay. *(to crew)* Let's get this show on the road.... Higher... get the damn thing up so I can read it... okay.... How do I look??... Let's go... *(sits in chair, composes himself, and beams a big, big smile, lights brighten considerably, simulating television lights)*... Tansi Saskatchewan... as leader of the Eagle Party, I am pleased to inform you that we are preparing to soar into the Twenty-First Century, to challenge tomorrow, and to take our rightful place as Aboriginal peoples in this great nation.... The Eagle Party has unveiled a plan that will declare war on poverty and unemployment.... No longer will our people be forced to live under a system of welfare that is unfair and degrading. A vote for the Eagle Party is a vote for freedom....

Join us and honour us with your vote January 15, 1995 as we enter a new dawn of change and prosperity.... Let us be your guide into the future and the new tomorrow... *(trails off, issues a disgusted laugh)*.... Cut!! *(lights return to original state of scene)* I think I'm gonna be sick... who writes this stuff ... a new tomorrow... give me a break... *(stands up and moves toward the camera)*.... Where's Frank?? We need some changes here... now!! *(hears telephone)* Hold that thought.... Yeah... oh... Mom... Mom... I can hardly hear you... howdja get this number anyways?? Oh nothing.... How are you?.... No, I can't make it this Christmas... I just can't do it.... I have to be in Ottawa.... What?... You're moving? Where? Dog Lake? ... Why?... Mom, listen to me, you can't move there, they're going to flood the whole damn... oh hold it... I've got another call... Mom, I'll have to call you back... Hello.... Oh, hi, honey *(takes pills out of pocket)* No, I just can't make it... I'm tied up here.... Look, it won't kill you to take the kids to the concert yourself.... *(to crew)* Hang on to your pants... *(to phone)*.... Look, we've been over this crap before... this isn't the time to discuss it, give the kids a kiss for me and *(wife hangs up in his ear)* Hello... hello... oh for crying out... hello... Mom... oh, I'm sorry... thought you were someone else.... No!!... nothing's wrong.... Listen, Mom... do me a favour, don't make any decisions about moving to Dog Lake until I get back to you, okay?... I'll call you back, I promise... *(embarrassed)* I love you too.... Good-bye... *(stands off to side, facing the singer, swallows pills, she frowns, he quickly looks away)*.... *(to crew)* One minute... *(dials number)*.... Yeah... Jack... is that Hydro still going through at Dog Lake??? Never mind why... I don't pay you to ask questions ... okay... I want to know immediately about anything that happens up there, you understand? Listen, Jack, one more thing... call Maryann and tell her to pick up the tickets to Honolulu.... Tell her I have to go to the kid's concert... she'll understand.... Oh what the hell... send her a dozen roses... that should do it... right *(hangs up)*.... Let's see *(squints at TV idiot card, puts on glasses, puts them back in pocket)* What have we got???... Okay, gentlemen... let's roll it.... Hold it

... lift that card up ... what do you think I am, a damn owl or something? *(television lights up)* Tansi Saskatchewan, as leader of the Eagle Party, I am pleased to inform you that we are prepared to soar into the Twenty-First Century, to challenge tomorrow, and to take our rightful place as Aboriginal people in this great nation.... The Eagle Party has unveiled a plan that will declare war on poverty and unemployment.... No longer will *(breaks up)*.... Oh cut, cut, I can't do this! ... This is stupid! *(starts to stride off, stops, sniffs the air)*.... I smell bannock.... Do you ... I'm going crazy!... *(exits)*

Scene Five

Silence. Then we hear the sound of a hand drum slowly pulsing a rhythm and the sounds of darkness. Lights come up on an Indian man behind a podium. On the podium are a number of microphones from various television and radio stations. He is wearing a traditional ribbon shirt with beaded designs. On his wrist is a beaded band. In his hair is an eagle feather hanging loosely on his chest. Around his neck is a necklace with a bone wolf.

MAN: Tansi, Glah na teh ... ah neen ... how ... welcome ... today is an important day for the Indian tribes of Saskatchewan and the rest of Canada. I have been given the honour of delivering a message from the council of elders.... It is hard for me to deliver this message as it contains pain and sorrow, but yet we are carrying a burden that must be lifted, words that must be spoken. After years of intense deliberation and negotiation with the Federal and Provincial Governments of Canada, the Indian tribes of Saskatchewan have made a final decision *(pause)* ... to break away from the rule and control of the dominion of Canada. Deliberations have taken a long time and every possible alternative has been explored in an attempt to avoid this decision to leave the confederation of Canada. We, as Indian people, claim sovereignty to the area of Saskatchewan extending from Cold Lake in the West to Amisk Lake in the East and including the territory of the

13

Amisk Lake in the East and including the territory of the Northern boundaries of Saskatchewan. This area is roughly half the province of present-day Saskatchewan. This land will remain as it always has been, as Saskatchewan. We see no reason to change the original Cree name given by our forefathers. From this day forward the territory known as Saskatchewan will be governed according to the customs and laws of the tribal councils of Saskatchewan. All those who wish to enter Saskatchewan will be required to submit an application to the Cree Nation Department of Immigration. All those who presently own or lease property in this territory are hereby given thirty days to relocate. All claims for compensation will be pursued with the appropriate government agency. The laws of the new Saskatchewan have been determined by the council of elders and they state that Indian languages are the official languages and the tribes of the First Nations will be asked to refrain from speaking other languages until such time as their original tongue returns. Televisions, radios, books, stereos, and other technological devices will not be permitted in Saskatchewan. Storytelling, dancing, singing, sports, and conversation will be the culture. Housing will be available for all. Transportation will be limited to medical and security personnel. A major hospital will be centrally located and medical doctors will work alongside Indian spiritual leaders in every community in the territory. We are confident that we can eliminate a number of diseases that we believe result from an unhealthy environment and lifestyle. The most essential healing process will be time. We have adequate food supplies and will continue to trade with other nations. We have a firm commitment to the gradual elimination of the monetary system and will base our livelihood on the traditional customs of sharing and co-operation. We have an adequate supply of fresh water and have made arrangements to insure that all families in Saskatchewan have their needs met in shelter, food, and water. All those who wish to live with the Indian tribes of Saskatchewan will be extended a sincere invitation to learn the languages and customs of Saskatchewan. As our forefathers welcomed shall we, only this time by the unwritten laws of the Cree, Dene, Saulteaux, Dakota, and Assiniboine. This message contains words of celebration and happiness as well as regret. I have chosen the words of the English poet, Matthew Arnold, with which to leave this society.... "For the world, which seems to lie before us like a land of dreams, so various, so beautiful, so new, hath neither joy, nor love, nor light, nor peace, nor certitude, nor help for pain, and we are here as on a darkling plain, swept with confused alarms of struggle and flight, where ignorant armies clash by night." ... Now, I invite you all to join me in a prayer to the Creator, regardless of your religious convictions... we ask for your guidance and we ask for courage and strength to travel this journey to our new world... we will always love you. Key ga sahg he hit tin nun. Meegwetch. Thank you, Kiche Manitou.

The MAN *bows his head and removes the eagle feather from his hair, then slowly raises the eagle feather up to the "sky." As the feather is being raised, the woman begins the song "Kayās Nehiyaw." The lights go down on the man and come up on the woman. Another spotlight comes up on the empty chair and the man walks across the stage slowly after removing the traditional clothing, the shirt, wristband, and necklace. When he reaches the seat, all that remains from the man behind the podium is the feather. He resumes his position of the dreamer in the seat. When the song ends, a messenger delivers a bannock wrapped in a cloth to the woman. She puts down her guitar, stands, accepts the bannock and walks over to the sleeping man. She gently positions the freshly-made bannock under the nose of the sleeping man.*

MAN: *(opens eyes)*   Bannock!! I knew I could smell bannock! *(gets up excitedly)*.... You wouldn't believe this dream I had!! I was a bum on the street and then I was teaching at the university and...

WOMAN: Where did you get the eagle feather?

MAN: *(just notices feather)* ... I don't know.... But I think I'll keep it.

Laughs, lights down.

END

by Winston Wuttunee

Kayās Nehiyaw kī-papamipiciw
Ita e-mīweyihtahk kī-mānokew
Kayās kīmīwāsin askīy
E-kī-pe-ohci-pemācihohk
Paskwāw mostoswak
Hi, Hi, Hi,

Nīya Nehiyāsis ninanaskomon
Kihceyihtetāk kiNehiyawewininaw
Kihceyihtetāk ōma askīy
Kā-tipeyihciket e-kī-mīkoyahk
Hi, Hi, Hi,

Niyā Nehiyāsis hi, hi, hi

A long time ago the Indian lived a nomadic life
Wherever he felt comfortable or balanced
There he would set his teepee
A long time ago the Earth was beautiful
His livelihood was the buffalo

I am an Indian   I am grateful
He was grateful for his Indianness
preserved with culture, with dignity
He was respectful to our Mother Earth and her sacredness
It was a gift from the Creator
For the Indian to use

PARTIAL LYRICS TO "BUFFALO JUMP"
by The Seventh Fire

What does it take to be a chief anyways?
Warning all nations buffalo jump ahead
The buffalo jump of the 1990s
What is the strategy and where is it leading?
Whoa, whoa, buffalo jump
I want to be right and I want to be free
No one's gonna come and terminate me
No one's gonna come and dictate to me
Look at the faces of the kids in the street
Their minds are blank and their future's bleak
They want to be right and they should be free
But something seems to keep getting in the way
Remember your history and then you'll understand
You may think I'm just an idiot
But listen to what I say
The system's illegitimate
I want to be right and I will be free
And that's why they can't intimidate me
Freedom is something that you will have to do for yourself

LYRICS TO "SAD MAN"
by Bruce Sinclair

The still of the night wakes him inside
He sees the dark deep in his heart
Sad man where are you going?
Are you moving too fast?
Sad man take some time
You're living your life for somebody else
One day you will sleep and never wake up
Your life will be wasted
Your song will be gone
Sad man you know you can't go on

GLOSSARY

sōniyās . . . . money (Cree)
Kayās Nehiyaw . . . . The Cree, of the past (Cree)
Kōhkum . . . . Grandmother (Cree)
Michif . . . . the Metis Language (Cree)
tansi . . . . hello, hi (Cree)
glah na teh . . . . a greeting (Dene)
ah neen . . . . a greeting (Saulteaux)
key ga sahg he hit tin nun . . . . we'll always love you (Cree)
meegwetch . . . . thank you (Ojibway)
Kiche Manitou . . . . The Almighty, Creator
or God (Cree)

The Park

Geoffrey Ursell

THE PARK IS MY FIRST PLAY, WRITten while I was living in an old apartment building in Winnipeg. One spring day, from my third-floor window, I watched the man who owned the house next door cut down, and then cut into pieces, a couple of very tall elm trees. The branches, then the trunks of the trees, thudded to the earth. His chainsaw roared all day.

Nearby was a very small park, tucked away from main streets and very quiet. It was a truly pleasant place to sit and read. And to think about the idea of "progress" – the destruction it seeks to justify and those who serve it – and the power of passive resistance.

These issues are more than ever a part of our lives: consider the attack on the rainforests of the world, on the old growth forests of British Columbia. Consider the way people resisted this attack at Clayoquot Sound.

But is that kind of resistance enough? Will the roar of the lion disguised as a cat continue to be heard?

Geoffrey Ursell is an award-winning writer of drama, fiction, poetry and songs. His first novel, *Perdue*, published by Macmillan in 1984, won the prestigious *Books in Canada* First Novel Award for that year. His plays, including *The Running of the Deer* and *Saskatoon Pie!* have won three national awards. Geoffrey has also written drama for radio and television, and he has composed songs and music for many plays by other writers. His first book of poetry, *Trap Lines*, was published by Turnstone Press in 1982. A second collection, *The Look-Out Tower*, also from Turnstone, appeared in 1989, as did a collection of short stories, *Way Out West!* from Fifth House.

At present, Geoffrey is working on a new novel, a collection of poems and a small-scale opera, with music by Rob Bryanton. Geoffrey was born in Moose Jaw, Saskatchewan, in 1943, and grew up in various prairie cities. He received his M.A. from the University of Manitoba and his Ph.D. from the University of London, England. He and his wife, writer Barbara Sapergia, both write full-time in Saskatoon.

Premiere Production

The Park won first prize in *Performing Arts in Canada* magazine's national Playwriting Competition, First Play Category, in 1972. It was first produced by Central Collegiate in Moose Jaw, Saskatchewan, directed by Wayne Dirkson, with Howard Glassman as the Dweller.

Characters

DWELLER: *Female or male, about twenty years old, dirty sneakers, dusty blue jeans and a grimy, bulky sweater.*

A CAT: *Male or female, played by an actor.*

CALLER: *Female or male. Slightly older than the* DWELLER *and more solidly built. Wears a snappy suit, highly polished shoes, glasses, and carries a leather portfolio case.*

DOCTOR: *Male or female. Fifty-five or so. Plump but not obese. Has a mellow voice.*

YOUNG LOVERS: *Female and male.*

OLD MAN OR WOMAN: *Wears old-fashioned executive dress. Evidently retired.*

CAT INSPECTOR

PARK INSPECTOR

PARK USE INSPECTOR

PARK CLEARANCE INSPECTOR: *Female or male. All of the above are dressed in dull-green identical uniforms. The only difference is the official name tags on their caps.*

WORKERS: *Male or female. In work clothes.*

Set Description

SCENE ONE: *A large room in an old apartment building that is being demolished. There are chunks of plaster from the ceiling and walls lying on the floor and plaster dust everywhere. There are* two doors, one near the back of each of the opposite walls. The door on the right side opens inwards (its handle is on the right-hand side) from a hall; the door on the left opens inwards (its handle is on the left-hand side) from the outside air. There is a cot, covered by a dusty grey blanket, against the back wall, equidistant from the doors. Hanging on the back wall, off-centre to the left, is a large calendar, with the month of May showing beneath a beautiful scene of mountains and water. Against the left wall is a three-drawer bureau. To the right front is a small, battered table and an old, rickety, bentwood chair. There is a worn, green rug covering all the floor.

SCENE TWO: A small park, dominated by a large tree trunk somewhat back from centre. The tree trunk may be as realistic or as stylized as the Director wishes. It could be hinged at the place where it's to be cut, and made to appear to start to fall by means of a rope attached to the top. The chainsaw is obviously not a working model – just a tape of its sound will do. In front of the trunk is a wood and metal, green park bench. The grass is the worn, green carpet from Scene One, upon which rests a slightly curving, black plastic path. There is a metal trash barrel to the left and a stone water fountain to the right. The park is surrounded by high brick walls, broken only by open-door exits from the path. No sky shows.

Scene One

The play opens with the DWELLER *sitting at the table holding an old, ragged but still serviceable umbrella over him/her and his/her plate while he/she eats cold beans with a bent fork from a chipped plate and drinks water from a chipped teacup. After a while he/she puts down his/her fork, picks up a few beans in one hand, bends down – while still trying to hold the umbrella over himself/herself and the meal – and throws them under the cot to the* CAT.

DWELLER: Here puss, puss. Here pussy! Have some beans. Share and share alike. *(Thud! goes something against the building, and the walls shake. Bits of plaster fall from above, and some bounce off the umbrella. A cloud of dust floats down. The* DWELLER *sits up quickly, protecting his/her meal. He/She fans the dust away and speaks to the* CAT *again.)* Now if you want any more, come right out and meow. There isn't much left, but if you want some.... *(the* CAT *meows mournfully)* Now I mean that, hear! We're in this together, remember. You didn't even have that much when I took you in. Saved you from those mangy curs. So no complaining. It's a lovely day out. Maybe we'll go for a walk in a little while. How's that with you? *(*CAT *meows somewhat more cheerfully)* Okay hey? Good. Eat your beans, then, and shut up.

He/She continues the meal with evident enjoyment. There is a firm knock at the right door, and the CAT INSPECTOR *opens it and peers around the door.*

INSPECTOR: Hello there. I'm the Cat Inspector. I'd like to see your license.

DWELLER: *(without turning)*   I'm sure you would.

INSPECTOR: You don't have a license then?

DWELLER: Well, I suppose I could find one somewhere. *(pulls out a wallet and looks through it, muttering)* Birth license... social insurance license... non-driver's license.

INSPECTOR: If you don't, I'm afraid it means severe penalties.

DWELLER: Of course. Do come in. Won't you all come in.

INSPECTOR: No. They can wait, thanks.

INSPECTOR *enters, closing the door behind him.*

DWELLER: A license... hmmm....

INSPECTOR: *(pulls out a package of cigarettes)* Do you mind if I smoke?

DWELLER: Go right ahead.

INSPECTOR: Thanks.

INSPECTOR *marches forward to the table, looks disdainfully at the beans, and returns the cigarette package to his pocket.*

DWELLER: *(looking up)* You know, we could ask the cat.

INSPECTOR: Ask the cat?

DWELLER: Yes, I'm sorry, but I simply can't remember where the license is. And it is the cat's license. *(beckons to the* INSPECTOR *to bend down, and whispers loudly in his ear)* Besides, I have a pathological fear of cats, not of talking to them of course, not even of leading them around... but touching them... *(makes a face)* Bleuhhh! And the cat might not answer unless it's stroked.

INSPECTOR: You must be crazy.

DWELLER: Yes, but I'm sure the cat's perfectly sane. Aren't you, cat? *(*CAT *meows affirmatively)* Go on, then, ask away.

INSPECTOR: Where is it?

DWELLER: *(aside)* Why do they always pick those with the dullest noses to be Cat Inspectors? *(turning back)* Under the bed.

INSPECTOR: *(faces cot, stands erect, clears throat)* Cat! Oh, cat!

DWELLER: *(in a conspiratorial tone)* I don't think it'll talk to strangers without seeing them first.

INSPECTOR: Oh. Well, I suppose I'd better see it too. *(walks over to the cot, gets down on hands and knees)* Because, if your case has been misrepresented, there could be serious consequences.

DWELLER: That's it. Bend right down. It's tied to the corner of the cot.

INSPECTOR: I don't quite see it. It's very dark under there.

DWELLER: It's all right. The cat sees you. Now, go ahead and ask.

INSPECTOR: Okay cat? Where's the license? *(the* CAT *lets out a shattering lion-like roar. This is immediately followed by a large Boom! from outside, which sends more plaster and dust tumbling from above. The* INSPECTOR, *who has recoiled onto his/her back, is showered with the dust. He/She gets up shaking, pulls a large rubber stamp from his/her pocket, and thuds it against the mattress. Then, remembering what seems to be under the bed, he/she jumps, says "Whoops!" and makes for the right door, thudding the wall with his stamp as he/she goes, saying)* Approved.... You're approved. Yes. Yes. Approved.

He/She turns and goes quickly out the door, closing it speedily but quietly. The DWELLER *returns to his/her meal, finishes, stretches back in the chair.*

DWELLER: Aahhh!

There is a brisk, hard knocking at the right door.

DWELLER: *(to himself/herself)* Hmm, must be noon. *(He/She folds up the umbrella and lays it on the table. He/She turns and calls out)* I'm here. Come in if you want to.

The right door opens and in strides the CALLER, *who firmly shuts the door, looks around the room, looks at the* DWELLER, *who has turned once more to face front, and looks again around the room.*

CALLER: Nice place you've got here, very nice indeed.

DWELLER: Suits me.

CALLER: Very nice indeed. Especially that calendar. *(looking at calendar)* Very nice.

DWELLER: I have a fondness for it, I must admit.

CALLER: Yes, very nice. But it's a bit wrong you know. Today, according to your calendar, the seventeenth, is a Sunday.

Now, I don't work Sundays, that's a certainty. In fact, today's Thursday. Only one more day of work. And that's sure. So your calendar, I'm afraid, is wrong. Incorrect.

DWELLER: Oh, I know.

CALLER: You know. Had it for a long time then?

DWELLER: Before I came here.

CALLER: And when was that?

DWELLER: I don't really remember.

CALLER: Hmm. But the month. I mean to say, the month is the right month, no doubting that... yes, it's May... then June ... then July, and my holidays. Three weeks of relaxation. We're taking the kids to Disneyland this year. All the way down to California. Three weeks. *(muses for a few seconds)* However, this month, May, the months are all torn off up to it but May looks like it's never been torn off. Never. Now why, could you tell me, is that?

DWELLER: I like May.

CALLER: Good, that's very good. That does explain the situation extremely well. Very well indeed. And it's been that way for how long?

DWELLER: I can't recall.

CALLER: But since before you leased this room?

DWELLER: Yes, and longer.

CALLER: But that's really most confusing, you know. Let's see. I'll just check that. *(He/She pulls out a billfold and consults a calendar card)* Ah, yes, just as I thought. You have another week, another seven days, until your lease expires. *(the* DWELLER *picks up the plate and licks it clean)* You know, you're not really being reasonable about this. After all, it's only seven days until you have to move anyway. And we've got a lovely apartment block just five minutes away... the same neighbourhood almost... everybody else, all your friends, your neighbours, were happy to go.

DWELLER: *(politely but firmly)* I think I'll stay.

CALLER: *(paying little attention)* Now we have just the suite for you. Two rooms, your own bathroom....

DWELLER: *(questioning but not interested)* One of the two?

CALLER: No, no, two rooms *and* a bathroom. Your own. No peeking out of the door in the morning to edge out the people next door. No waiting in line. Ha, ha. None of that. Your own private bathroom. Yes, I think that's more than fair. And rent-free for the first month, and after that the same as you're paying here. Exactly the same. Two rooms *and* a bathroom. *(firmly)* Now *do* be reasonable.

DWELLER: Thank you no, thank you yes.

CALLER: Thank you no, thank you yes to what?

DWELLER: Thank you no, I'm staying; thank you yes, I'm reasonable. Or vice versa. Whichever you prefer.

CALLER: Prefer! *(slightly disgusted)* You're costing us five thousand a day while you stay here. Five thousand a day.

DWELLER: You shouldn't have started so soon.

CALLER: Nonsense. We had to start when we did in order to finish on time.

DWELLER: But you won't anyway.

CALLER: Won't what anyway?

DWELLER: Won't finish... on time, anyway.

CALLER: We will if you'll only cooperate. If you'd try to understand our position. If you'd realize that it's inevitable ... sixty-two stories right here.

DWELLER: And....

CALLER: And what?

DWELLER: And the park. The park is part of the right here, isn't it?

CALLER: Well?

DWELLER: Thank you yes, thank you no. Or vice versa.

CALLER: Hmm... well, I can see you're adamant. Like a rock. But I have something of a surprise for you... something of a surprise.

DWELLER: Really? My birthday's not till January. And I'm not married, so that rules out anniversaries. And I don't think I'm about to die... unless... so you can't be throwing a wake for me. Mind you, if that is the case, you're welcome to attend.

CALLER: No, no, no. Nothing like that, nothing like those. This is a surprise in human form, living form.

DWELLER: That may be. The corollary in this case isn't a necessary function of the axiom.

CALLER: Another caller, that is. I'm sure you'll like him *(or her)*. And I'm sure he'll *(or she'll)* understand you. I left him *(or her)* just outside. Do you mind if I invite him *(or her)* in? I'll go and get him *(or her)*. *(He/She does not wait for an answer, but walks over to the right door, opens it, and calls out)* Doctor! Oh, doctor! Sorry to have kept you waiting. Would you like to come in now? *(He/She turns back to the DWELLER)* The Doctor was just looking through the ceiling. He *(or she)* has a perceptive mind, a very perceptive mind.

DWELLER: *(to no one in particular)* And there are holes in the ceiling.

CALLER: *(not listening)* A perceptive mind.

The DOCTOR enters.

CALLER: Well, there he *(or she)* is, Doctor.

DOCTOR: Ah, yes.

DWELLER: A perceptive mind.

CALLER: So if you'll just excuse me, I'll leave you with him *(or her)* for a while. I'll be down the hall. When you're finished you can call me.

The CALLER leaves, closing the right door softly behind him/her.

DOCTOR: May I sit down?

DWELLER: Oh, you may. But I'm using the only chair, as you may see, and the bed's quite dusty... though solid enough I should imagine. So you may, but you probably won't.

DOCTOR: But I shall just turn back the cover of your bed.

DWELLER: If you wish. However, I had better warn you that there is only one sheet beneath that cover, and the water has been turned off for six weeks. I had nothing in which to save water, and the laundromats in this area charge exorbitant prices. Consequently, that sheet has not been washed for almost two months. You can draw your own conclusions. But do turn back the cover if you want. I have no desire to be inhospitable in any way. In fact, having considered the matter with due care and alacrity, I am now prepared to offer you my chair, in proper deference to your benign years and apoplectic appearance. *(He/She rises)* Do sit down.

DOCTOR: Thank you, I will. Thank you indeed. *(He/She sits)*

DWELLER: *(assuming a professional air)* Now, what is your problem?

DOCTOR: Well, to be perfectly truthful about the matter, I suppose my problem is you. You may have already guessed, hardly perceptively, that I have been retained by this construction – post-demolition, to be sure – by this construction firm to discuss with you the possibility of your vacating these premises before your lease expires. They have assured me, following my inquiries into the situation, that legal action has been fully considered and found impossible. You are in the right... legally... but it is felt that you are not giving due consideration to several other factors that are inextricably involved.

DWELLER: This is a problem, isn't it? You want me, as you so quaintly put it, to vacate my premises. Let's begin with this, then. When the law serves morality, should morality desert the law? Shall we proceed?

DOCTOR: Thank you, but I'm rather hesitant to pursue that line of reasoning.

DWELLER: Yes, it is insecure ground. That I must admit. And the historical trend has been, as you must know, against the mixture… the intellectual trend of interpretation, that is.

DOCTOR: The proper relationship of one's ideals to the material world I cannot pretend to be able to show you. We must live as we must live.

DWELLER: Precisely. Would you like something to eat? *(He/She goes to the bureau, opens the second drawer, pulls out a can of beans and displays it to the* DOCTOR*)* I was saving this for a special treat, but since you've come at this time I do feel obliged to offer you something.

DOCTOR: Really, you mustn't feel obliged to offer me anything. As a matter of fact, I have already had my lunch.

DWELLER: Ah, I see. But wouldn't you like a snack, to tide you through until supper? *(places the first can of beans on top of the bureau, closes the second drawer, opens the third and pulls out another can of beans)* Perhaps a little of this. *(repeats action, closing the third and opening the first drawer)* Or this. *(repeats actions, closing the first and opening the second drawer)* Or this. You see, I have quite a selection of delicacies. Enough of a selection, I should imagine, to tempt the most refined of palates.

DOCTOR: But those are all beans, all cans of beans.

DWELLER: So *they* say. And, further, what do you mean by "all beans"?

DOCTOR: Hmm. *(pulls a small notebook with a leather cover from his/her inside suitcoat pocket and makes a note)*

DWELLER: Yes… hmm. However, since my bounty doesn't tempt you, may I ask if there is anything else you would like?

DOCTOR: Well… well, I do have a test I would like you to take. Here. *(pulls a folded sheet of paper from the notebook)* Yes, I'm sure that this will prove both interesting for you and profitable for me. You see, all you have to do is put a checkmark in one of these squares, any one at all. There are three squares, you see, beside each number, and fifteen numbers. Here's a pen. *(offers his pen)* This shouldn't take long. Here. Just checkmark one of these squares for each number.

DWELLER: Yes, I see. No questions to answer. Just check off a square for every number. All right. *(does the test rapidly)* There you are. *(hands back the test and pen)*

DOCTOR: Thank you, thank you very much. Now if you'll let me correct it. I won't take long. I can do it right here.

As the DOCTOR sits correcting the test, the DWELLER goes to the bureau and puts the cans back in their respective drawers. He/She then moves around the room, examining the pieces of furniture carefully, as if weighing their relative positions in his/her mind. The DOCTOR grows more and more perplexed as he/she continues to correct the test. He/She makes short notes in three or four places as he/she proceeds. After a while he/she speaks.

DOCTOR: This is really quite strange, quite strange, not to say most perplexing.

DWELLER: Oh?

DOCTOR: You got every one wrong. Every answer is wrong.

DWELLER: *(contrite)* I never was any good at tests… of any kind. I confess that without any qualms of conscience, without any qualms at all.

DOCTOR: But really, how do you expect the test to help me if you get all the answers wrong?

DWELLER: I am sorry. But as I've already confessed, I never was any good at tests. I think that it must be obvious now to both of us that I'm still no good… obvious indeed. But I'm willing to try again. No hard feelings. I will try again.

DOCTOR: No. No. I don't think that would help anything. But these results are most perplexing. However… all is far from lost. This will make a most interesting paper for presentation at the next meeting of the Society… a most interesting paper.

DWELLER: Well, I'm glad I could help in some way. Now, would you mind doing me a favour?

DOCTOR: *(musing)* Yes, I can see the excited faces now ... What's that? A favour? I suppose I should, shouldn't I?

DWELLER: Oh, don't feel obligated to me in any way.

DOCTOR: No, no, of course not. What kind of favour?

DWELLER: Get up.

DOCTOR: Why, certainly. *(rises)* Is that all?

DWELLER: Thank you. Now if you'll excuse me for a minute.

The DWELLER *proceeds to move the chair and table from right front to left front, leaving the* DOCTOR *musing over the test. He/She then carries the bureau to an opposite location on the right wall, then moves the calendar from the nail it is hanging on to another nail on the other side of the back wall. He/She surveys the scene and then sits down in the chair.*

DWELLER: There, that does it.

DOCTOR: *(still musing)* Yes ... yes ... one could come to some startling conclusions.

DWELLER: *(catching* DOCTOR'*s attention)* Thank you, Doctor. Would you care to continue our discussion now?

DOCTOR: No, no, thank you anyway. I must get back to my office.

DWELLER: Well, goodbye then. It was pleasant meeting you.

DOCTOR: Thank you. Thank you. Goodbye.

The DOCTOR *wanders over to the right door, opens it, and leaves. The* DWELLER *goes over to the bureau, opens the top drawer, and takes out an already open can of beans. He/She walks back to the table, empties out the few beans that are in the can onto his/her plate, walks back to the bureau, opens the third drawer, and puts the can in. He/She walks back to the table, sits down, and begins to eat.*

DWELLER: *(murmuring)* Delicious, delicious.

There is the sound of firm footsteps in the hall, and the CALLER *comes in brusquely, slamming the door behind him/her.*

CALLER: *(angrily, but still in control)* That was neatly done. My congratulations. I told them that a doctor wasn't going to help. But they said it was the only civilized alternative left.

DWELLER: *(calmly continuing to eat)* Civilized alternatives are rather limited.

CALLER: Yes, aren't they. *(submerges his/her bitterness for a moment under a facade of reasonableness)* But really, I simply don't see why you're refusing to move. This isn't any fun for me, you know. I'd just as soon be shaking your hand in welcome to your new apartment as go through this.

DWELLER: Well, I'd hate to call you obtuse. So let's just say it's a matter of principle. But I am staying.

CALLER: Principle. We're losing five thousand a day and you're sitting here on your principle. My God, some principle!

DWELLER: You know quite well that your God has little enough to do with my principle.

CALLER: *(very angry)* Staying! Staying. *(threatening)* For seven more days you're staying. And then, you're out. I've damn well played around with you long enough.

DWELLER: *(calmly)* I've had that pleasure for six weeks.

CALLER: Well, I haven't, I don't, but I will. Then it's lights out. Lights totally out!

DWELLER: Say, I've been meaning to thank you for that. It was almost providential. I would have liked to offer you a drink, but since my water's been cut off I have to carry it up from the fountain a cupful at a time. But at least you haven't kept me in the dark. Knocking down that wall *(gestures towards front)* was very kind. And the southern exposure, too. Sunlight all day. The moon and stars at night. It's almost like camping out. Why, I remember –

CALLER: Damn it! Damn it! You even like that. What a job. What a stinking job. Why can't we just smash the whole mess down? Oh, it'd come down fast enough with a few

33

smashes from our machine. But with you up here, we have to be careful. If we hurt you – that's it. We lose the contract. We'll probably lose it anyway with you sitting up here on the stupid fifth floor. So don't tempt us, just don't tempt us.

DWELLER: Well, thank you anyway. For the view. Thank you indeed.

CALLER: And you say "thank you." Okay. That's it for today. Game over for today. I'm leaving now. But I'll see you tomorrow. And every day, every day until next Thursday. When out you go *(enunciating clearly)* right out on your butt, my friend, right out on your butt. So, goodbye.

The CALLER *turns to go out the right door, but notices that the furniture contradicts that choice. So he/she walks over to the left door, opens it a little, all the while looking at the* DWELLER's *back. The* DWELLER *is apparently enraptured by the audience. The* CALLER *pulls a final disgusted face and goes out very quickly. The door is jerked shut forcibly and suddenly, as if someone falling had been holding on to it.*

DWELLER: *(returning from his/her memories at the noise)*   Well, time for our walk, eh, puss? *(He/She rises and goes over to the left door)* It looks like a lovely day out. *(He/She throws the door wide, revealing the sky, and sunshine streams in. The sound of bird songs is heard, and a light breeze blows into the room)* And it is a lovely day out. Look. Beautiful. *(He/She walks away from the open door, bends down to unleash the* CAT*)* Come on, puss. I think we'll go for a stroll in the park.

The DWELLER *leads the* CAT *to the table, picks up the umbrella, and goes out the right door. After a moment something goes Thud! against the building, the walls shake, and bits of plaster fall and dust floats down.*

An uptempo version of "April Showers" plays as the INSPECTORS *and the* WORKERS *rush on, transforming the apartment into the park as quickly as possible.*

Scene Two

The DWELLER *enters from the right, swinging the furled umbrella. He/She walks over to the trash barrel and the* CAT *climbs into it.*

DWELLER: There we are, cat. Stay in there now. Out of harm's way.

The CAT *meows in agreement. The* DWELLER *dusts his/her hands together, puts the umbrella under an arm, and walks back to and sits down in the middle of the bench, all the while humming the tune of "April Showers." He/She may throw in some gestures to the unsung words. There is a large buzzing, as of a portable chain saw, which grows in volume during the song. Finally, a large, sawn-off branch falls near the trash barrel with a great crash. The* CAT *lets out a frightened meow.*

DWELLER: Stay in there, cat. It's safest. Just let me enjoy the fresh air and sunshine.

The DWELLER *relaxes with his/her legs stretched out. He/She begins humming again. Two* YOUNG LOVERS *enter, one from each side, reaching out their hands to one another. They come down the path, kneel at opposite ends of the bench, and move forward, still with outstretched arms, gazing rapturously into one another's eyes. They meet in a long embrace over the* DWELLER. *A* PARK INSPECTOR *enters from the right, carrying a checklist on a clipboard.*

INSPECTOR: *(stops by the fountain and reads from list)* "One drinking fountain. Davis Foundries. 1931. Connected by Waterworks Crew Number Six, W. Cross, Foreman, July 23, 1932." *(makes a check mark)* Check. *(walks over to bench, reads from list)* "One bench. Adanac Manufacturing Company Limited. 1947. Repainted 1949, 1959, 1969, 1979, 1989, with Standard Park-Bench Green. Serial Number" *(bends down to look under right end of bench)* … no, not there. *(walks behind bench to other end, bends down)* No, not here. *(crawls under bench below trio on it)* Ah, yes, underneath this paint. *(pulls out a paint scraper from jacket pocket and scrapes away)* Number… "Number 549 Z22 1A7." *(makes a check mark)* Check. *(gets up, walks over to*

trash barrel) "One trash barrel. Williams Foundries. 1985."
A good year for barrels. *(fondles metal rim. Looks in. Without
surprise)* What's this? A cat? The things some people throw
away. One trash barrel. *(makes a check mark)* Check. Seems
to be all. I'll phone the crew. *(exits left)*

The YOUNG LOVERS *break up their embrace. They relax like the*
DWELLER, *one on either side of him/her, and hold hands across
him/her. They join in the hum. An* OLD MAN/WOMAN *enters from the
left, walks to the barrel, searches in it, pulls out a newspaper. He/She
pulls a long piece of gum out of his/her mouth and puts it in the
newspaper and wads it up. He/She dumps it back in the barrel. He/She
belches. He/She walks over to the bench, surveys it, and sits down
beside the girl or boy. The buzzing begins again and another branch
thuds to the ground right behind him/her. He/She is startled, turns to
look, gets up and goes over to examine the branch. He/She mutters
"Humph!" and returns.*

The PARK USE INSPECTOR *enters right, carrying a clipboard.*

INSPECTOR: A lovely day for using the park. And how many take
advantage of that fact? Few. Pitifully few. The dregs of society,
and that's about all. *(addresses the* OLD MAN/WOMAN*)* You,
my good man, *(or woman)* how often do you visit this park?
More than enough, I'm sure.

OLD MAN/WOMAN: *(disgruntled)*   Clean it up! Clean it up! You'll
triple your annual turnover! Triple it! Clean it up, I say!

INSPECTOR: That's not my department. *(to himself/herself,
making a check mark on the clipboard)* Casual visitor.
Check. These others. Young lovers. Casual. Obviously.
Infrequent casual. Check. *(starts to walk by bench.* DWELLER
gets up, follows behind INSPECTOR, *who walks over to the
trash barrel, looks in)* Humph. Casual. Check. *(He/She turns
and bumps into the* DWELLER*)* What are you doing in my
way? Obstruct a Park Use Inspector, would you?

*Short saw buzzes followed by small branches falling all over the stage
– except on the people – break into the succeeding speeches, and may
force the speakers to shout.*

DWELLER: I wish my use to be recorded.

INSPECTOR: I'm sure you would. Well, that's my responsibility. To record Park Use. Where were you hiding? You must have been hiding.

DWELLER: I use this park, and twenty-six others, each day and every day.

INSPECTOR: Each day and every day? What do you mean? Which branch of the Parks Department do you work for?

DWELLER: No branch.

INSPECTOR: Then who do you work for?

DWELLER: Everyone. But not all the time.

INSPECTOR: Well... unemployed, eh? I have no category for you. Hence, no interest. Can't record you. Your use doesn't count. Now *(walks around and away from the* DWELLER*)* ... I must get on with it. *(to self)* This one can go. No use. No use at all. And look at this artificial turf. *(kicks at the rug)* How scruffy. And this path. *(stomps on it)* Cheap, very cheap material. An obsolete model. Quite obsolete.

The PARK USE INSPECTOR *exits right. The* DWELLER *follows him/her as far as the fountain, stops there, pulls out a teacup, fills it and drinks. Branches fall near and on him/her. He/She unfurls the umbrella and raises it. He/She returns to his/her place on the bench between the* YOUNG LOVERS. *The* YOUNG LOVERS *and the* OLD MAN/WOMAN, *now being littered with small twigs, snuggle closer to the* DWELLER, *crowding their heads underneath the umbrella. Larger branches fall behind them. The* PARK CLEARANCE INSPECTOR *enters right, ringing a school bell and speaking through a bullhorn.*

INSPECTOR: Clear this park. Clear this park. Disperse in an orderly fashion. Disperse in an orderly fashion. The police cordon will not detain you if you leave immediately. No questions will be asked. Clear this park. *(exits left. There is a brief silence. Suddenly he/she re-enters, walking from left to right, swinging the bullhorn to all points of the stage)* Clear this park. Clear this park. Disperse in an orderly fashion. Disperse in an orderly fashion. The police cordon will not detain you if you leave immediately. No questions will be asked. Clear this park. *(He/She stops in front of the bench and addresses the* YOUNG LOVERS *through the bullhorn. The* OLD MAN/WOMAN *has fallen asleep during the announcements and sagged down on the bench. The heads of the* YOUNG LOVERS *are in front of and obscure the face of the* DWELLER*)* Excuse me, have you… whoops! *(turns off the bullhorn)* Excuse me, have you seen an uncategorized person here? I have to validate his departure. *(the* YOUNG LOVERS *shake their heads)* No? *(walks away)* Well, it was worth a try. Their dreams may have crossed. But if there's one thing I hate about this job, it's trying to track down uncategorized people. Usually impossible, of course, quite impossible.

The YOUNG LOVERS *rise and exit right. There is a brief silence. The* DWELLER *gently awakens the* OLD MAN/WOMAN *with a hand on his/her shoulder.*

DWELLER: Better clear out. They're renovating the park.

OLD MAN/WOMAN: Humph! Needs it. Triple their turnover. Triple it, I say. *(exits right)*

The PARK INSPECTOR *enters right, followed by two* WORKERS.

INSPECTOR: *(consulting clipboard)* "One fountain." Check.

He/She points to the fountain and the WORKERS *rip it up. They carry it off right and quickly return.*

INSPECTOR: "One bench." Check.

As the WORKERS *move, one to each end, the* DWELLER *stands. They lift the bench straight up and carry it off right. The* DWELLER *sits back down on the ground.*

INSPECTOR: "One trash barrel." Check. *(makes hurried gestures to the returning* WORKERS*)* Pile in some of those branches, boys.

The WORKERS *grab some branches and shove them in the barrel. There are a few piteous meows. The* DWELLER *sits with his head bowed underneath the umbrella. They carry the barrel in front of him off right.*

DWELLER: Sometimes you just can't help it. Inexorable. Finally inexorable.

INSPECTOR: What else? *(looks around.)* Oh, the path. Hey, don't forget, the path.

The WORKERS *return, rolling up the path as they come. They carry it off right.*

INSPECTOR: Might as well leave this turf. Pretty worn out. Unless. And… whoops! One tree. Almost forgot. Come back, boys. One tree. *(yells up at the tree top)* Hey! Stop that now! Pull your saw back into the building. That's right.

The WORKERS *return. One of them carries a portable chainsaw.*

INSPECTOR: Lay it this way, boys. *(points to audience)* It'll be easier to pick up. No one's in the way.

The PARK CLEARANCE INSPECTOR *enters right. He/She speaks through the bullhorn to the audience.*

PARK CLEARANCE INSPECTOR: All clear. All clear. For park renovation. All clear.

The WORKERS *start the saw. They go to the back of the tree and begin to saw there. The* PARK INSPECTOR *and the* PARK CLEARANCE INSPECTOR *move one to each side of the stage and look up towards the invisible tree top. The* WORKERS *pull the saw away.*

WORKERS and INSPECTORS: TIMBER!

The tree cracks and creaks as it begins to topple forward, down upon the head of the DWELLER. *Suddenly everything freezes. The tree hangs suspended. There is complete silence. The lights slowly go to black. An old recording of "April Showers" begins to play.*

END

Me 'n' Alfred

Beechy High School Drama Club

ME 'N' ALFRED WAS AN ADVENTURE, to say the least. When we were first asked if we wanted to be in a collective creation, none of us had any idea what a collective creation was! When we found out it meant writing and acting out our own play, we quickly got excited about the idea. We were told that our teachers were there only as supervisors, and that all the work had to be done by us. It wasn't long before we found out the reality of how difficult writing a collective play was really going to be.

We agreed on a theme pretty quickly, but then we spent a long time improvising scene after scene. The next part was very frustrating – narrowing down the scenes and coming up with an incredibly rough draft of what would become *Me 'n' Alfred*. Even after we had the script, the play went through constant changes. The actors developed their characters more and more, which meant the play developed in different ways each day.

After a lot of after-school and weekend rehearsals, *Me 'n' Alfred* was finally ready to be performed. What makes this play unique is that it is not the work of one person, but rather the creation of fourteen different people, under the watchful eye of two directors. It is an equal effort made by all, and it couldn't have been done any other way. —*Steve Labelle, student and collective member*

The members of the Beechy High School Drama Club collective that created *Me 'n' Alfred* are: Les Covey, Raelyn Dorward, Kim Erickson, Stephanie Erickson, Michael Hanke, Lorena Hanson, Theressa Houben, Noel Jansen, Mike Labelle, Steve Labelle, Chad

Smith, Shelley Stenerson, Angela Unger, and Christine Woelk. Several cast members also helped to create "Joyride" and "Instant Replay," the Drama Club's next two plays.

Me 'n' Alfred was the Beechy High School Drama Club's first venture into the collective creation process. We have continued doing collective plays, the students growing in the arts, and growing as problem-solving and caring human beings. The birth of *Me 'n' Alfred* was a school exercise, an education.   —*Larry Warwaruk, teacher*

I've worked on a lot of plays, but *Me 'n' Alfred* will always be close to my heart. All of the students worked hard – with honesty that was often startling, on their own time, and *together*. Their collective voice comes through loud and clear. I'm glad I was there to see it all happen.   —*Glenda MacFarlane, supervisor*

CHARACTERS

BUM (SHELDON MITCHELL #1): *He is in his forties, but looks older. He wears a battered hat and layers of old and dirty clothing. He's been living on the streets for more than a year, begging and scrounging money for booze. He begins the play with a hangover, and gets drunker and drunker as the play progresses.*

SHELDON MITCHELL #2: *He is Sheldon #1 seen in flashbacks. His costumes may change between scenes, as his life changes.*

SANDRA CORY MITCHELL: *Sheldon's wife. She is a strong woman whose life also changes throughout the course of the play.*

DARREN MITCHELL: *Sheldon and Sandra's son. He is fourteen.*

RCMP OFFICER: *A middle-aged cop. He has seen it all.*

MR. MITCHELL: *Sheldon's father. A real party animal.*

JESSICA MITCHELL: *Sheldon and Sandra's daughter. She is sixteen.*

LOUISE: *Sheldon's sister, who is the wedding M.C.*

WAITRESS: *A young woman who works at the bar.*

JACK DUNCAN: *One of Sheldon's drinking buddies.*

IMPY: *The bartender at Sheldon's favourite watering hole.*

BELINDA: *A prostitute in Sheldon's hometown.*

JILL SANDERS: *Sandra's best friend.*

ANGEL: *Belinda's friend.*

MRS. MITCHELL: *Sheldon's mother.*

MRS. CORY: *Sandra's mother. A classy woman.*

MICHELLE: *Sheldon's grad escort.*

JUSTIN: *A high school friend of Sheldon's.*

MR. CORY: *Sandra's father. He is quite wealthy.*

BUBBA: *The bouncer at the bar. She is tough.*

A DRUNK: *One of the bar patrons.*

The following roles may be doubled:
Darren/RCMP Officer/Mr. Mitchell; Jessica/Louise/Waitress;
Jack/Impy; Belinda/Jill; Mrs. Cory/Michelle; Justin/Mr. Cory/
A Drunk.

Set Description

*Staging should be kept as simple as possible. Boxes may be used to
represent furniture, and scene changes should be minimized.
Cross-fades, rather than blackouts, should be used between scenes.*

Scene One

New Year's Eve in a prairie town. The stage is dark. In the distance, a town clock begins to strike 11 PM. Lights come up slowly on a refuse-littered alley. As the clock continues to strike, the BUM *begins to stir beneath a pile of newspapers. He has been passed out on a makeshift pallet of an old suitcase, papers, perhaps an ancient stained mattress.*

The BUM *shakes off the papers, rises painfully to a sitting position, and holds his head. We see that the* BUM *is wearing filthy and ill-fitting clothes – perhaps a pair of stained polyester pants, shoes with holes in them, or a dirty raincoat with sleeves that are too short. On his head he wears a battered hat with a distinctive band. He begins to cough, a racking cough that goes on and on. He leans over, coughs up phelgm and spits. The* BUM *then reaches for his whiskey bottle, which is lying on the ground. He discovers that the bottle is empty.*

Shakily, he begins to search for another bottle, which he has hidden, but he can't remember where he put it. He looks for it, reaching down into his pile of garbage, pawing through papers on his hands and knees. He can't find it, and panics.

Finally he looks at a large rusted garbage can. He pauses for a moment, and then dives into the garbage can, pulling out garbage and scattering it around. He pulls out a full bottle of rye. The BUM *cradles it in his arms for a second. With shaking hands, he twists the cap off. He smells it, sighs with relief. He tries to raise it to his mouth, but his hands are shaking so hard that he's afraid he'll spill some of the precious liquid. He breathes, tries again. The* BUM *manages to drink from the bottle this time, a long draught that warms him, brings him back to life. He drinks again. His symptoms are disappearing now, and he's gaining confidence. At last, he seems to notice the audience. He addresses the audience.*

BUM: Oh. It's you, Alfred. Haven't seen you around here in a long time. How've you been? *(pause)* What? Not talking? Nothing to tell? Well, come on over here, then, and I'll tell you about me. (BUM *sits on his pile of junk. Leans back, relaxes. His speech is slightly slurred)* Life's been real fine. No rules. No more nagging from that wife of mine, and all the freedom a man could want. I've never been better off. (*pause*) My wife did me a favour when she kicked me out, she did. (*pause*) Yes, she did.

The BUM *pulls a harmonica out of his coat pocket and plays a few notes on it. Lights fade on the* BUM. *However, the* BUM *remains on stage throughout the action, sometimes watching the action, sometimes sleeping.*

SCENE TWO

A telephone rings. Lights up on the Mitchell house living room. SANDRA, *who has been dozing on the couch, picks up the phone. She is wearing a dressing gown and is clearly anxious. Unnoticed by* SANDRA, *her daughter* JESSICA *has heard the phone ring.* JESSICA *comes into the room, where she listens to her mother's conversation.*

SANDRA: Hello, Sheldon? (*pause*) In jail.

Lights fade as SANDRA *puts down the phone.*

SCENE THREE

SANDRA *is now in the kitchen, at the stove. She's slamming pots and pans around.* DARREN *and* JESSICA *are watching television in the living room.* SANDRA *burns herself on a frying pan and drops it with a clatter.*

SANDRA: Damn!

JESSICA, *in the living room, hears her mother, and goes into the kitchen. She comes up behind* SANDRA.

JESSICA: Mom, are you okay?

SANDRA: I'm fine; leave me alone.

JESSICA: But…

SANDRA: (*cutting her off*) Just go back to what you were doing!

JESSICA returns to the living room. SANDRA *sighs. She sits down at the kitchen table, puts her head in her hands. In the living room,* DARREN *is lying on the couch, still watching sports on TV, occasionally flicking the remote at the set.* JESSICA *gets up from her chair and paces. She accidentally ends up in front of the TV.*

JESSICA: (*to* DARREN) Dad phoned last night.

DARREN: Yeah, so what. Would you move, please?

JESSICA: He phoned to say that he was in jail.

DARREN: So what's new. You wanna eat this remote? Now move!

JESSICA: Poor Mom. You know, I wouldn't blame her if she left him. (*There is no response from* DARREN. JESSICA *pushes it a little further*) Dad would deserve it if Mom left him.

DARREN: (*sitting up*) Why is it always Dad's fault? Can't you see what Mom's doing to him?

JESSICA: What?! Mom hasn't done anything to him!

DARREN: She has so. She keeps pressuring Dad. She keeps trying to change him into something he's not.

JESSICA: Yeah?

DARREN: (*by now they are both standing, facing each other down*) Yeah!

JESSICA: You know why?

DARREN: Why?

JESSICA: Because Dad's an alcoholic! She's only trying to make him stop drinking.

DARREN: (*yelling now*) He wouldn't have started drinking if she hadn't got on his case in the first place!

SANDRA *is listening to their conversation from the doorway between the kitchen and the living room. Neither of the kids notice her.*

JESSICA: Oh yeah, that's right. You men stick together worse than glue. You're impossible.

DARREN: Look, all I'm saying is that none of this would have happened if Mom hadn't tried to change Dad.

JESSICA: And I still say Mom should leave him. (*pause*) I'm going to the mall.

DARREN: Good riddance!

JESSICA *leaves.* DARREN *flops back down onto the couch and fiddles with the TV. He turns up the volume and from the TV the audience hears, "I'm a Bud man, yeah, I'm a Bud man ...."* SANDRA *has gone from the kitchen to the bedroom. By the time the beer commercial has ended on the TV, she is in the living room, carrying two suitcases.* DARREN *turns the TV off.*

DARREN: What are you doing, Mom?

SANDRA: I'm just waiting for your father to come home.

DARREN: How come you packed bags?

SANDRA: Those are your father's.

DARREN: But Mom, you can't kick Dad out!

SANDRA: Don't tell me what to do.

SANDRA, *wanting to avoid a confrontation with* DARREN, *goes back into the kitchen and starts fiddling with the pots and pans again.* DARREN *is following her.*

DARREN: If you kick Dad out, then I'm going too!

DARREN *stomps back to the living room after this declaration. This time* SANDRA *follows him.*

SANDRA: Don't be ridiculous! You're not going anywhere!

SHELDON #2 *enters through the front door. He is well-dressed, if somewhat rumpled after his night in jail. He wears a hat, recognizable as the same hat the* BUM *wears, only now it is new. He doesn't notice the suitcases in front of the door and falls over them, flat on his face. There is a moment of stunned silence.*

SHELDON: What's with the bags on the floor?

SANDRA: Darren, go to your room. I want to talk to your father.

DARREN *looks at his mother, then at his father. He exits.*

SHELDON: Well, is someone going to tell me what the bags are for?

SANDRA: They're for you.

SHELDON: Why? Where am I going?

SANDRA: Look, I don't care where you go. I just want you out of my life.

SHELDON: What do you mean?! How are you going to get me out of your life when we have two kids?

SANDRA: I've had to raise those kids on my own. The only time you're around is to take them to the mall or to a stupid ball game.

SHELDON: Bullshit! That's not true. Who do you think brings in the money to pay all the bills?!

SANDRA: Half of the money that you bring in goes toward booze.

Pause. SHELDON *knows that, this time,* SANDRA *is serious. He takes a minute to sit on the couch. When he speaks again, he is conciliatory.*

SHELDON: Look, I'm sorry, but can't we patch things up? If you think that I'm drinking too much, I'll stop. I promise.

SANDRA: No. I've had enough of your promises.

SANDRA *turns her back on* SHELDON *and starts toward the kitchen. He begins to come after her.*

SHELDON: But...

SANDRA: *(turning suddenly)* Please. Don't make it hard. Just... leave.

SANDRA *goes into the kitchen, sits at the table, begins to cry.* SHELDON *stands for a moment in the empty living room. He looks slowly around the house, then picks up the bags and leaves, as the lights fade.*

Scene Four

We hear music on the harmonica, perhaps a few bars of "Cigarettes, Whiskey and Wild, Wild Women" or "There's No Place Like Home." Lights up on the BUM *as he plays. He is drunker than he was in Scene One. He continues to get drunker as the evening wears on.*

BUM: Hey, Alfred, got a smoke? *(There is no response)* Come on, buddy, have a heart. Fine then. I'll just find one myself. *(The* BUM *grubs around in the debris until he finds a long butt under some of the debris. He lights it, the flare of his lighter nearly setting his hair on fire. He settles back down onto his pile of junk as we hear the sound of a siren screeching down a nearby street. He laughs.)* Some guy's wife isn't gonna be happy when she gets a call from the station. Nailed me for impaired driving once. Thought I was drunk!

Lights fade on the BUM *until all we see is the glow of his cigarette in the dark.*

Scene Five

BUBBA'S VOICE: Next time you'll get the tree!

Lights up on SHELDON, *who has just been thrown into a parking lot, obviously very drunk. His hat comes flying out toward him. He picks it up.*

SHELDON: Up yours, Bubba!

He starts peering at cars, trying to focus his eyes. At last he looks in the window of one, decides it's his, and begins fumbling in his pockets.

SHELDON: Keys, keys, keys...

He pulls the keys out of his pocket with a jerk. His hat falls off. He picks up his hat.

SHELDON: Where is that damn thing?

He's looking for the lock on the door. At last gets the door open. He gets in and slams the door. He attempts to get the keys in the ignition, but drops them on the floor. He bends down, picks them up, and whacks his head on the steering wheel on the way up.

SHELDON: Ouch!

SHELDON *starts the car. It dies. He starts it again, stomps on the gas and roars the engine. The radio is on.* SHELDON *puts the car into gear and steps on the gas, taking off with tremendous speed and nearly giving himself whiplash. He goes around some curves, listening to the radio. A smarmy song comes on.*

SHELDON: Ugh.

He begins to turn the tuning dial of the radio. We hear static, maybe a Labatt's ad, more static. SHELDON *hits the dashboard a couple of times. Then, one hand on the steering wheel, he bends over and starts fiddling with a radio wire. After a second, he takes the other hand off the wheel and fixes the radio. A horn honks. He looks up, hauls on the wheel to get back in his own lane.*

SHELDON: Whoa!

On the radio, SHELDON *locates a song from his youth, perhaps "Light My Fire" by The Doors. He turns the volume up and beats to the music on the steering wheel. We hear the wail of an approaching siren.* SHELDON *looks in the rear-view mirror.*

SHELDON: Some idiot's in big trouble tonight.

SHELDON *looks in the mirror, back at the road, back in the mirror – a double-take.*

SHELDON: Shit!

SHELDON *pulls over to the side of the road. He puts his hand in front of his mouth, smells his own breath. An* RCMP OFFICER *approaches the car, flashlight in hand. He taps on the window of* SHELDON's *car.* SHELDON *waves to him.* COP *motions for him to roll down the car window.*

SHELDON: Aah, is there a problem, ossifer?

COP: Yes, you were clocked doing seventy kilometres an hour in a fifty kilometre zone. So could I see your license and registration, please?

SHELDON: (*reaching for his wallet*) I'll co-operate in any way, sir.

SHELDON *has leaned too close to the* COP, *who catches a whiff of* SHELDON'*s breath.* COP *winces.*

COP: Excuse me, sir; could you step out of the car for a second and walk along the yellow line.

SHELDON: Is there a per-roblem, sir?

COP: Just step out of the car, please.

The COP *opens the car door and* SHELDON *falls out on the ground. He gets sick on the* OFFICER'*s shoes. The* COP *grabs him, throws him up against the car.*

COP: You're under arrest!

Lights snap out.

Scene Six

We hear SHELDON *singing "Nobody Knows the Trouble I've Seen... " Lights come up on the police station.* SHELDON *is sitting on a bench between two women who are apparently prostitutes,* ANGEL *and* BELINDA. *He has one arm around each of them and is singing his heart out.*

COP: Hey buddy. We'll give you one call, and if it doesn't work, you're in the drunk tank all night.

SHELDON *staggers over to the* COP'*s desk.*

SHELDON: Watch this.

SHELDON *gives the phone receiver a karate chop with one hand, and catches it in the other hand.* COP *shakes his head.*

COP: Give me that. I'll call for you. What's your phone number?

SHELDON: 859-2...

COP: (*dialling*) Yeah?

SHELDON: 859-20 ... (*He honestly can't remember*)

SHELDON: (*starting again*) 859-20...

COP: Come on, I haven't got all night.

SHELDON: 859-206... (*He is distracted by a framed photograph on the cop's desk*) Hey, is this your mother?

COP: No, that's my wife. The number!

SHELDON: 859-2060.

The COP *hands* SHELDON *the receiver. He listens for a moment, then...*

SHELDON: Hi, honey. Guess where I am...

Lights down.

Scene Seven

We hear a song, perhaps "I've Got Friends In Low Places" playing. Lights up on the BUM.

BUM: Hear that music, Alfred? (*He listens for a moment*) It's coming from Nicki's Place. You remember that place, don't you? (*pause*) What do you say we go in, for old time's sake?

BUM *gets up and walks down steps off the stage, across the floor to the other side of the stage. He walks up steps and into the centre of the stage, which is set up as a bar.*

BUM: (*turning and motioning to audience*) Come on.

The BUM *walks to the back of the bar and slumps down at one of the tables. Lights and music fade. The* BUM *exits in the black.*

Scene Eight

Lights up on Nicki's Place again. Now several people are sitting at tables, drinking. Nicki's is not a high-class joint. IMPY, *the bartender is pouring drinks which a* WAITRESS *is slapping unceremoniously down onto tables. One of the downstage tables is overturned, and a* DRUNK *is lying on the floor beside it.* BUBBA, *the bouncer, is standing over top of the man, holding a baseball bat. We hear* SHELDON *and* SANDRA *talking as they enter the playing area on the floor in front of the stage.*

SHELDON: Whaddya mean, dirty?

SANDRA: Dirty! You heard me. I'm not going in that… that… rat-infested sewer!

SHELDON: Sewer! What, do you think you're too good to go in?

SANDRA: I…

SHELDON: Little Miss Perfect! All your life, nothing's too good for you. Fine, sit out here! I don't really care.

SANDRA, *almost in tears, goes back the way they came.* SHELDON *goes up the steps to enter the bar. As he opens the door,* BUBBA *has managed to wrestle the* DRUNK *to his feet.*

DRUNK: Leggo! You don't know who you're dealing with…

BUBBA *grabs him by the collar and hurls him out the door, as patrons in the bar chant "Bubba! Bubba!" The* DRUNK *falls down the steps onto the floor, narrowly missing* SHELDON.

SHELDON: What the…

The DRUNK *picks himself up and staggers off, muttering.*

SHELDON: *(to* BUBBA*)* Wha'd he do?

BUBBA: He messed with the tree.

SHELDON: What tree?

BUBBA *goes over to the tipped-over table and picks up the baseball bat. She walks menacingly back to* SHELDON *and brandishes the bat.*

BUBBA: You mess with me, you get the tree.

BUBBA *hits the palm of her hand with the bat a couple of times to make sure* SHELDON *gets the message. Then she leaves him, to set the table back up.* SHELDON *shakes his head, then crosses to the bar to order a drink.*

SHELDON: *(to bartender)* Who's she? And who was the loser she threw out?

IMPY: That's Bubba Bruiser – the best bouncer in *(the name of your town)*. As for the drunk, well, some guy I've never seen before. *(He hands* SHELDON *a drink)*

SHELDON: Thanks. Okay, well, I'll be sure to stay out of her way.

IMPY: The name's Impy. Bubba's all right. She just has a little communication problem. She hates everyone.

SHELDON *laughs, then leaves the bar and sits down at a table. He quickly downs his drink and motions for the* WAITRESS *to bring him another one. The lights fade; music is heard; time passes. When the lights come up to full again,* SHELDON *is very drunk. Empty glasses litter his table. His jacket is off and his hair is disheveled. We hear a popular raunchy song, as if on the jukebox.* ANGEL *and* BELINDA *cross the floor in front of the stage and climb the steps. They enter the bar, walking past* SHELDON *to sit at one of the tables.*

BELINDA: Look at that poor sap.

ANGEL: Yeah, just one too many. He's probably an easy target.

BELINDA: Yeah, but you can never be too sure. I'll ask Impy.

BELINDA *goes to the bar and consults with* IMPY. IMPY *shrugs his shoulders.* BELINDA *gives* ANGEL *an okay signal.* ANGEL *crosses over to* SHELDON. *He doesn't realize she's there. She puts her hand on his shoulder. With a start, he sees her. She sits down and puts her arm around him.*

ANGEL: Hi honey. You all alone tonight?

SHELDON: Sorta.

ANGEL: Why, what do you mean?

SHELDON: My, uh, wife… she's… wai–

SANDRA *enters the bar in time to see* ANGEL's *arm around* SHELDON.

SANDRA: Sheldon!

SHELDON *stands up, almost knocking over the table.*

SHELDON: Ya finally came aroun'! C'mere baby. Have a drinnnnk!

SANDRA: I will not! Give me the keys.

SHELDON: *(fumbling for the keys)* Keys, keys... Hey, wai' a minnit! Wha ya wan' 'em for?

SANDRA: Oh never mind! I'll find my own way home!

SANDRA, *furious, leaves.* BUBBA *has been watching them as if expecting trouble, but* IMPY *restrains her from intervening.* SHELDON *flops back down into his chair.*

SHELDON: *(to* ANGEL*)* She left me! *(laughs)* She can't do that!

ANGEL: Huh?

SHELDON: *(in disbelief)* She left me, just left.

ANGEL: Well, baby, it happens. *(pause)* Say, let's go on upstairs and –

SHELDON: *(angry)* Why? You wanna know why? Because of this!

SHELDON *throws his half-empty glass across the room. It smashes on the floor. There is silence. Everyone stares at him.* BUBBA *grabs her tree and starts toward* SHELDON. ANGEL *motions for her to stop.* IMPY *restrains her.* ANGEL *pushes* SHELDON *back into his seat.*

ANGEL: Listen buddy! Calm down. Tell Angel where it hurts. What's your name?

SHELDON: Name? Na... Sheldon. Sheldon Mitchell.

ANGEL: Well, now –

SHELDON: I wasn't good enough for her. Nothing was ever good enough! I worked hard, right? Tried to provide for her, but that little –

ANGEL: Who are you talking about?

SHELDON: Sandra!

ANGEL: Sheldon, keep your voice down.

SHELDON: Don't tell me what to do! That's all she ever did.

ANGEL: But if you don't be quiet, Bubba will –

SHELDON: Do what? Kick me out?

SHELDON *stands up, purposely knocking over the table.* BUBBA, *bat in hand, starts toward him.*

SHELDON: C'mon Bubs! Jus' try it!

SHELDON *takes a swing at* BUBBA, *but misses her. She picks him up easily, and drags him toward the door. The other patrons in the bar begin chanting "Bubba! Bubba!"*

SHELDON: Hey! Let go, dammit!

BUBBA *tosses him down the steps of the bar. Lights down, quickly.*

Scene Nine

Lights up on the bar – the patrons are gone; the overturned table has been set upright; the BUM *is once more huddled at a table in the back.* IMPY *and the* WAITRESS *are closing up the bar.*

IMPY: *(to* WAITRESS*)* That's good enough. Go on, get out of here. It's New Year's Eve. Go find a party.

WAITRESS: *(exiting)* Thanks, Impy.

The BUM *crosses to the bar.*

BUM: Say, Impy... Could you... for old times' sake... Could you spare a drink?

IMPY *looks at the* BUM *with disgust, then hesitates a moment. He reaches under the bar and pulls out a nearly-full bottle of rye whisky.*

IMPY: Happy New Year. Now get outta here.

BUM: *(so overjoyed that he is almost incoherent)* Thanks... thanks.

Afraid that IMPY *may change his mind, the* BUM *leaves the bar quickly. Lights fade on the bar as the* BUM *crosses in front of the stage. The clock starts to strike twelve.*

BUM: (*holding out the bottle*) Hey Alfred! Want to help me bring in the new year? (*getting no response*) No? Well, that's more for me, then.

The BUM *shuffles up the other steps, back to his pile of junk. He settles down, has a couple of drinks as the clock finishes striking. At the last stroke of midnight, we hear party sounds – horns and voices shouting "Happy New Year!" Two couples, dressed up, with party noise-makers walk past the* BUM, *talking excitedly about partying. They meet, nearly in front of the* BUM, *recognize and greet each other. "Happy New Year!" they yell, and hug one another before they continue offstage.*

BUM: (*holding up the bottle*)   Happy New Year! Happy New Year!

The couples don't notice him. The BUM *has another drink.*

BUM: All this celebrating. Reminds me of my wedding. My old man sure enjoyed himself. Too bad he didn't know how to handle his booze. (*laughs*) My mother was really proud, even though she thought Sandra's family was so much better than us. Them and all their stinking money! (*pause, as he takes another drink*) Yep. It was a good day, though.

The BUM *plays a couple of notes on the harmonica and sings "Here comes the bride, short fat and wide" … Lights down.*

Scene Ten

Lights up on a wedding banquet head table. The audience is the rest of the wedding guests.

LOUISE: Welcome all honoured wedding guests and friends. And now I'd like to introduce you to the head table. To my immediate right you have the parents of the groom, Mr. and Mrs. Mitchell.

As each guest is introduced, he or she stands, and the others applaud.
MR. MITCHELL, *who is quite drunk, makes a big production out of bowing.* MRS. MITCHELL, *embarrassed, pulls him back into his seat.*

LOUISE: The best man, Jack Duncan.

JACK, *a good-time kind of guy, waves or holds his arms up in a "champion" pose to the audience.*

LOUISE: The man himself, Sheldon Mitchell.

JACK: *(yells)* Hoo-hoo-hoo!

LOUISE: The lovely bride, Sandra Mitchell. The maid of honour, Jill Sanders.

MR. MITCHELL *whistles at* JILL. MRS. MITCHELL *elbows him in the ribs.*

LOUISE: And the parents of the bride, Mr. and Mrs. Cory.

The CORYS, *a dignified couple, rise and bow politely.*

LOUISE: We will now have the cutting of the cake.

SANDRA *and* SHELDON *cut the cake.* MRS. MITCHELL *snaps three quick flash photos. Other wedding guests yell comments and make jokes to the bride and groom.* SANDRA *feeds* SHELDON *a piece of cake; it is a sweet moment – the guests say "Aww!" and applaud.*

LOUISE: The best man, Jack Duncan, will now make a toast to the groom.

JACK: Sheldon and I have been friends for a long time. I recall one party we were at. *(He pauses for a second and looks at* SHELDON, *grinning)* There's been quite a few parties. Anyways, there was a tattoo guy at this one party, and we were just teasing each other about getting a tattoo. We were saying things like "Who's man enough to get one right on the butt?"

SHELDON *can't believe* JACK *is telling this story. The* CORYS *look at one another with a bit of alarm.*

JACK: Well, Sheldon got up, staggered across the room and said, "I'll get 'I love Sandra' tattooed on my butt."

The other guests react strongly. MR. MITCHELL *thinks it's hilarious,*

MRS. CORY *is appalled, the others are variously amused or embarrassed.*

JACK: Well, I guess the tattoo guy had a little too much to drink – like the rest of us. Because he had a little problem spelling "Sandra."

Pause. MR. MITCHELL *is heard saying "Oh-oh… "*

JACK: And so, now and forevermore, it says on Sheldon's butt, "I love Santa."

The other guests laugh, some uproariously. Even MRS. CORY *allows herself a pinched smile.* MR. MITCHELL *nearly falls off his chair laughing. He spills his drink on* MRS. MITCHELL.

JACK: Raise your glasses for a toast to Sheldon Mitchell, my best bud.

ALL OTHER GUESTS: *(rising)* To the groom! *(They toast)*

JACK *sits down.* SHELDON *teases him, shaking his fist at him as if to say, "I'll get even with you!"*

LOUISE: The maid of honour, Jill Sanders, will now make a toast to the bride.

JILL: In all my years, I would never have guessed that these two would be getting married. I thought they were too different – but I guess this proves that opposites do attract. Sheldon and I were in the same graduating class, and since Sandra was a good friend of mine, she came to my grad. That's where they were introduced. Sheldon was a bit bombed, and had fallen straight back and passed out midway through the night… and the kind girl Sandra is, she went to his aid. She continued to be his Florence Nightingale in university; they spent quite a bit of time together and eventually fell in love. *(to* SHELDON *and* SANDRA*)* I hope you two have a great life. *(to guests)* Lift your glasses for a toast to the bride.

ALL OTHER GUESTS: *(rising)* To the bride!

LOUISE: Thank you, Jack and Jill.

MR. MITCHELL: Who went up the hill and bumped their head. Ha ha ha!

MRS. MITCHELL: Shh!

LOUISE: The dance floor is off to the left. Everyone have a great time, and – PARTY ON!

A slow dance song from the era begins playing. SHELDON *rises,* SANDRA *takes his arm and they lead the way to the dance floor. The other guests follow, except for* MR. CORY, *who remains seated.* MR. MITCHELL *crosses over to the bar to get another drink. He sees* MR. CORY *and sits on the table beside him.* MR. MITCHELL *takes a drink from his glass. Throughout the rest of the scene, music typical of wedding dances is heard.*

MR. MITCHELL: Haaah. Smooth! *(pause.* MR. CORY *tries to ignore* MR. MITCHELL)* Looks like the kind of wedding me and the old lady had a while back. Yup. But then the young'ns come and then the wife wants no more drinking. But hell, they can't run our lives! Nope, the man's got to be the boss.

MR. CORY: Yes. What is it that you do?

MR. MITCHELL: I make sure the wife stays in line and looks after the kids like she's s'posed to. Ha ha ha! Ah, I usually find the odd job between drinks. What d'you do?

MR. CORY: I own some businesses. If you will excuse me…

MR. CORY *stands up and walks away.* MR. MITCHELL *staggers off to the dance floor.* SHELDON *enters, en route to the bar.* MR. CORY *stops him.*

MR. CORY: Can I talk to you a minute? I want you to take that money and the job in my business. I – I want the best for my daughter.

SHELDON: I know you do, and I'm going to do my best to give it to her. I don't need your money or your job – like I said before, I'll do fine on my own. Your daughter will get the best. I've got a job, and I'll support her. *(pause)* I saw you talking to my father. Don't worry, I'll never become like him.

MR. CORY: I sincerely hope not, son. *(pause)* Remember, if you ever need anything, come to me.

SHELDON *and* MR. CORY *shake hands.* MR. CORY *exits to the dance floor.* SHELDON, *who is joined by* JACK, *goes to stand at the bar. We hear "Ob-La-Di, Ob-La-Da" by the Beatles.* MR. MITCHELL *and* MRS. CORY *dance onstage.* MR. MITCHELL *is now completely drunk and out of control. First he waltzes* MRS. CORY, *then twirls her around wildly and begins to two-step.* MR. MITCHELL *breaks away then and does the twist, and* MRS. CORY *tries to back away. He grabs her arm, pulls her to him, and they polka. At the instrumental break,* MR. MITCHELL *launches into a "Saturday Night Fever" disco-style dance. By now the others are watching and laughing, cheering* MR. MITCHELL *on. Once more,* MRS. CORY *tries to escape, but* MR. MITCHELL *lunges for her, and pulls her in close. As the song ends, they tango, and on the last "If you want some more, sing ob-la-di-bla-da!"* MR. MITCHELL *dips* MRS. CORY. *The other guests applaud and disperse.*

MRS. CORY: Umm, thank you for that interesting dance.

MR. MITCHELL *heads over to the bar.* MRS. MITCHELL, *mortified by her husband's conduct, takes* MRS. CORY *over to where the wedding gifts are piled, trying to do some damage control.*

MRS. MITCHELL: My, your daughter looks beautiful. Where did you find such a lovely dress?

MRS. CORY: Why, Sandra has only the best! Of course, it's a Paris design. Mine as well. And yours?

MRS. MITCHELL: Oh, I found it at some shop downtown on sale. It was a great price … But enough about clothes. I wonder when our first grandchild will come?

MRS. CORY: Not for a while, I hope. I want my daughter to be a successful businesswoman before she starts with the children. Why, she's only twenty. She was born when I was thirty, and even that was just about too early I think. When did you have your children?

MRS. MITCHELL: I had Sheldon's older sister when I was sixteen … My, these are lovely decorations… If you will excuse me, I have to go check on my husband…

MRS. MITCHELL *goes to find* MR. MITCHELL. MRS. CORY *picks up an armload of wedding gifts and moves them offstage.* JILL *and* SANDRA *rush in, talking excitedly.*

SANDRA: Guess what? I'm going to have a baby!

JILL: (*hugging* SANDRA) That's great! Congratulations!

SANDRA: I just found out about it – I haven't told anyone but you and Sheldon. So please don't say anything to my mother.

JILL: She can't run your life forever. I know Sheldon's mother will be happy; she loves children. And you and Sheldon will make great parents.

SANDRA: Sheldon's very happy. He says he's going to support me and the baby and he'll be the best father ever. He also says he won't hang out with the guys anymore, and won't spend all the money! You know, I think getting married and me having a baby is the best thing that could happen to him.

JILL: Me too. Oh, I just can't believe that you two are actually married! Remember the night of the grad?

SANDRA: Things have changed.

JILL: If you ever need me, to babysit or anything, just call me. I'll be there for you.

SANDRA: Thanks.

SHELDON *comes over to* SANDRA.

SHELDON: Are you ready to go, hon?

SANDRA: Yes. Just let me say goodbye to Jill.

SHELDON: Okay. I'll be right over there. (*He gestures to the bar*)

SANDRA: Well, I guess this is it!

JILL: I'll miss you.

SANDRA: It's not like I'm going away forever! I'll be back in a couple of weeks.

JILL: I know. I just get sentimental at weddings.

JILL *hugs* SANDRA *again.* SANDRA *gets* SHELDON, *and* JILL *goes to the dance floor.*

JILL: Hey, everybody! They're leaving!

All the guests gather around SHELDON *and* SANDRA, *and* JACK *organizes the throwing of the bouquet, which* JILL *or* LOUISE *catches.* JACK *then shouts "Garter, garter!" until* SHELDON *gets the garter from* SANDRA'S *leg and shoots it toward the guests.* MR. MITCHELL *gives the quarterback sack to all the other guys, knocking them out of the road, to catch it. The guests ad lib "Congratulations" and "Have a great time" and "See you soon," throwing confetti at* SHELDON *and* SANDRA *as they leave.*

MR. MITCHELL: Don't do anything I wouldn't do!

Lights snap out.

SCENE ELEVEN

Lights up on BUM *as he is zipping up his pants; he's been urinating against a wall in the alley. The sound of a car going past very fast, blaring a rock song.*

BUM: *(nodding in direction of the car and music)*   Kids! Off to another party, I suppose. *(He sits down at his usual spot, takes a couple of swigs from the bottle of whiskey)* I guess the best party I ever went to was my graduation party. I did graduate, you know, Alfred. Now that was a good time. At least, what I can remember of it. Don't remember much after I met Sandra...

Lights fade.

SCENE TWELVE

Music up, very loud; a popular song from the time of SHELDON'S *graduation, perhaps a Doors song. Sounds of a noisy party. Crash of bottles, yelling, cars driving up. Kids talking. Lights up on party scene. Groups of graduates are milling around, some in formal clothes, others in jeans. All have beer bottles in hand.* SHELDON *is at a table with* MICHELLE, *his grad escort. He is nuzzling her neck. As he reaches to put his hand on her breast, he knocks his bottle of beer onto her lap.*

She screams and stands up.

MICHELLE: *(trying to wipe the stain off her dress)* Sheldon, look what you've done!

SHELDON's friend JUSTIN *comes up behind him.*

JUSTIN: Maybe you should slow down, Sheldon.

SHELDON: What do you mean? That wasn't my fault, it was an accident.

MICHELLE: It was so your fault. You're drunk. Justin's right, you should slow down.

JUSTIN: *(reaching out to put his hand on SHELDON's shoulder)* Come on Sheldon, take it easy, eh?

SHELDON: Get your damn hands off me!

JUSTIN: Hey ...

SHELDON: Just mind your own business!

SHELDON *pushes* JUSTIN. JUSTIN *backs off, knowing* SHELDON *is very drunk.* SHELDON *pushes* JUSTIN *again.* JUSTIN *is getting angrier, but he still doesn't fight back.* SHELDON *slaps* JUSTIN *in the face.* JUSTIN *gets angry, and punches* SHELDON. *They fight for a few minutes.* SHELDON *gets in a few lucky hits, but* JUSTIN *eventually knocks him to the ground.* SHELDON *lies on the ground, groaning.* JUSTIN *shakes his head.*

MICHELLE: Sheldon, you're such a loser! I've had it – we're through.

MICHELLE *and* JUSTIN *leave the party together.* JILL *and* SANDRA, *who have been watching the fight, go to* SHELDON.

JILL: Sheldon, Sheldon. Are you all right?

SHELDON: *(as* JILL *helps him up)* Yeah.

JILL *notices* SHELDON *staring at* SANDRA.

JILL: I'm sorry – Sheldon Mitchell, this is Sandra Cory. She's been dying to meet you all night.

SHELDON: *(to no one in particular)* Man, single for five minutes and already the chicks are knocking at my door.

SHELDON *holds out his hand to shake* SANDRA's *hand. He's weaving back and forth. Just before* SANDRA *can shake his hand,* SHELDON *falls straight backward. He has passed out cold.*

SANDRA: Oh my God, Jill! What happened?

JILL: I don't know. (*She looks for his pulse, puts her ear to his chest*) Oh God, I don't think he's breathing!

SANDRA: What should we do?

JILL: You took first aid… give him mouth-to-mouth!

SANDRA *bends over and begins to give* SHELDON *mouth-to-mouth resuscitation. After a few minutes,* SHELDON *regains consciousness. He puts his arm around* SANDRA, *rolls her over and kisses her.* SANDRA *screams and jumps up.*

SANDRA: That was a quick recovery.

SHELDON: Man, that's the first time I ever woke up like that!

JILL: Sheldon, are you all right?

SHELDON: Yeah, just help me up and get me the hell out of here.

JILL *and* SANDRA *get on either side of* SHELDON *and try to help him up and out of the party. Just as they manage to get him moving toward the door,* SHELDON *puts his hand on* SANDRA's *rear end.* SANDRA *is startled and jumps away.* SHELDON *falls like a tree, passed out on the apron of the stage. Lights snap out.*

Scene Thirteen

Lights up on the BUM. SHELDON *is barely visible, still passed out. The* BUM *is now very drunk. He stares out at the audience.*

BUM: Where are you going, Alfred? What, you don't like my company? Aw, you'll be back. You just can't stand to see me living so good, can you? Well, tha's no… problem…. Just go find myself some more New Year's cheer….

The BUM *stands up, staggers across the front of the stage until he's beside the prone figure of* SHELDON, *although the* BUM *doesn't appear to see* SHELDON. *The* BUM *takes the last drink from his bottle, and lays it gently beside* SHELDON's *body. He then steps over* SHELDON, *and walks across the stage. He turns to the audience.*

BUM: Happy New Year, Alfred.

The BUM *walks upstage into the shadows, singing "Should auld acquaintance be forgot, and never brought to mind...." Lights fade to black.*

END

Wheel of Justice

SUNTEP Theatre

AS STUDENTS AND STAFF AT
Prince Albert's Saskatchewan Urban Native Teacher Education
Program (SUNTEP), we meet once a week as SUNTEP Theatre. Our
goal, as teachers and teachers-to-be, is to provide a positive and
celebratory voice for our program and for Aboriginal people in
general. For this reason we create children's theatre out of legends and
stories, from Wīsahkecāhk to Robert Munsch. These are performed
at schools in and around Prince Albert. All of our plays are collective
creations; they grow out of discussion and improvisation by
students and staff. *Wheel of Justice* was no exception. The play was
essentially scriptless in the conventional sense; it changed from
performance to performance. It was only after many performances
that it was transcribed from video tapes for the writing of this script.

We believe that theatre is a language that we can use to respond
to issues of concern to Aboriginal people. For that reason, we invite
Aboriginal and non-Aboriginal students alike to read and perform
this play. *Wheel of Justice* is our irreverent response to the
quinticentennial celebrations that were held in 1992 to
commemorate the arrival of Mr. Columbus on this continent. We
hope you enjoy it as much as we did.

—*Lon Borgerson, SUNTEP teacher*

SUNTEP Theatre's plays are collective creations and deal with issues
that concern Aboriginal people. "The Great Canadian Golf Crisis"
(1990) was a response to the Oka situation and to the issues of land
rights and self-determination. It was performed at the World
Indigenous Peoples' Education Conference in New Zealand, in
1990. "Silent Voices" (1993) is a video-drama about family violence
which is being used extensively in workshop venues. SUNTEP

Theatre has also created numerous children's theatre productions for schools in the Prince Albert area.

SUNTEP is a teacher education program for students of Aboriginal ancestry, and SUNTEP students bring with them a rich variety of cultural and community backgrounds. The 1992 cast of *Wheel of Justice* was no exception: Marie Whitefish (Big River Reserve), Alice Parenteau (Duck Lake), Josie Nicolas (Duck Lake), Brenda Seidler (Prince Albert), Eva Sylvestre (Dillon), Kevin Lavallee (Prince Albert), Cheryl Arcand (Muskeg Lake), Prisca Jennett (Christopher Lake), Patty Herriot (Christopher Lake). Nearly all of the cast are 1994 graduates of SUNTEP and the University of Saskatchewan College of Education. At the date of this publication, Lon Borgerson, Murdine McCreath, and Michael Relland continue to teach at the Prince Albert SUNTEP Centre, and to work with SUNTEP Theatre's latest collective creation, "Family Feudalism."

Premiere Production

Wheel of Justice was performed by SUNTEP Theatre in the spring and summer of 1992 at the following locations: SIAST – Woodland Campus; Gabriel Dumont Institute Human Justice Program; Saskatchewan Drama Association Provincial Festival; Indigenous People's Writers Festival (Duck Lake); Joe Duquette High School/Coalition 500 (Saskatoon); Saskatchewan Penitentiary; Riverbend Institution; International Indigenous Youth Gathering (Little Red Park); Saskatchewan Teachers Federation Guidance Counselling Conference; Saskatchewan Teachers Federation Work Experience Conference; Pinegrove Correctional Institute; Gabriel Dumont Institute Annual Cultural Conference; and SUNTEP. The final cast was as follows:

STAGE MANAGER	Lon Borgerson
WĪSAHKECĀHK	Marie Whitefish
DEFENCE	Alice Parenteau
PROSECUTION	Josie Nicolas
COURT RECORDER	Brenda Seidler
BAILIFF	Eva Sylvestre
JUDGE	Kevin Lavallee
CHRISTOPHER COLUMBUS	Michael Relland
NINA	Murdine McCreath
PINTA	Cheryl Arcand, Prisca Jennett
SANTA MARIA	Patty Herriot
TECHNICIAN	Ron Fines

Characters

STAGE MANAGER: *Male or female.*

WĪSAHKECĀHK: *Male or female. An androgynous type. Dressed in black, face painted and hair braided. Feather in hair.*

DEFENCE: *Male or female. Wearing a red robe.*

PROSECUTION: *Male or female. Wearing a red robe.*

COURT RECORDER: *Male or female. Gaudily, but simply, dressed.*

BAILIFF: *Male or female. Wearing a dark blue commissioner's uniform.*

JUDGE: *Male or female. Wearing a black judge's robe.*

CHRISTOPHER COLUMBUS: *Male. Wearing a multi-coloured pompadour, a flowing golden cape, a frilly white shirt, black tights, white socks, and a lot of jewellery.*

NINA, PINTA, and SANTA MARIA: *Male or female. Dressed as human ships.*

Set Description

The stage is dominated by a large wheel of fortune, three quarters of it painted one colour and labelled in glittering letters "not guilty." The pie-shaped slice that is left is labelled "guilty." In front of the wheel is the judge's table, covered in red cloth. The court recorder will sit to the right of this desk. The defendant's chair is to the immediate left. Tables for the prosecution and defence are further forward, angled towards the audience. At the very edge of the stage, on one side or the other, is a set of traffic lights.

Scene One

STAGE MANAGER *enters from side of stage that traffic lights are on.*

STAGE MANAGER: Ladies and gentlemen, if I could get you to take your seats please. Quickly if you can, then we will get started. I have some important things to tell you for the success of this trial and for this evening of television. Now, a few important things you have to know before we start televising this court session. We need your co-operation. Here is the first thing. At a certain point during the show, I am going to cue you. I am going to say, "Ladies and Gentlemen, it is the moment you have all been waiting for. It's... " and I want everybody to shout three words. And the first word is "Wheel."

AUDIENCE: WHEEL!

STAGE MANAGER: With feeling, with feeling now. All right, now let's try that again.

AUDIENCE: WHEEL!

STAGE MANAGER: Try to do it at the same time as everybody else. That was good. The second word is... "of!"

AUDIENCE: OF!

STAGE MANAGER: The third is... "justice."

AUDIENCE: JUSTICE!

STAGE MANAGER: Now let's try it again. Together. Ladies and gentlemen, it is the moment you have all been waiting for. It's...

AUDIENCE: WHEEL! ... OF! ... JUSTICE!

STAGE MANAGER: That's magnificent! Give yourself a hand, ladies and gentlemen. Absolutely wonderful, wonderful! Now, when the moment comes, we need everybody just to belt that out, just as loud as that. Raise the whole city of (*your town*). Make them all wake up. Now listen, here's the other thing folks. At a certain point, these lights are going to come on up here. When the green light comes on, we want cheering and whooping and lots of applause.

Green light comes on and the AUDIENCE *cheers.*

STAGE MANAGER: When the yellow light comes on, we want polite applause.

Yellow light comes on and AUDIENCE *applauds lightly.*

STAGE MANAGER: There was a little bit too much feeling. Try again.

AUDIENCE *applauds lighter.*

STAGE MANAGER: When the red light comes on, we want booing and hissing.

Red light comes on and the AUDIENCE *boos and hisses.*

STAGE MANAGER: If you really want to get into it and yell things like "Hang him! Hang him! String him up by the... !" Anything like that, go right ahead. Let's try it again.

AUDIENCE *boos and hisses and yells.*

STAGE MANAGER: I think we got her. We got her. One last thing, when all three lights go on, at certain points of the program, you are going to be filled with excitement and you are going to break into a spontaneous wave. Everybody will stand and whoop at the same time. It will start at this side over here. All three lights.

All three lights come on at once. AUDIENCE *does the wave.*

STAGE MANAGER: A little shaky over here. Let's try it again. Let's get the whoop all the way across. Go.

AUDIENCE *does the wave again.*

STAGE MANAGER: Watch for all three lights at the same time. Okay, ladies and gentlemen, I think we're ready to begin.

As he exits the red light comes on and the AUDIENCE *boos and hisses.* STAGE MANAGER *responds with a rude gesture. Flute music:* WĪSAHKECĀHK, *the Trickster, peeks from behind the wheel. She moves mysteriously and curiously into the courtroom, almost dancing with* slow, stylistic movements. *From table to table she moves, sits in the* JUDGE's *chair, inspects the gavel, the papers, then back to the wheel. She touches and caresses the wheel, then grabs it with both hands and spins it hard. A wild hubbub erupts, with actors entering the courtroom as journalists, TV and radio broadcasters, interviewers, all jockeying to do their own "one-man shows." As the noise peaks,* WĪSAHKECĀHK *stops the wheel. The actors freeze.* WĪSAHKECĀHK *smiles. She slowly turns the wheel backward and the actors move and speak "in reverse." They are rewound off the stage in slow motion. A moment of silence and* WĪSAHKECĀHK *grabs the wheel and spins it again, harder this time. As the wheel whirls, loud circus music erupts and then the amplified voice of the* STAGE MANAGER *is heard.*

STAGE MANAGER: Yes, Ladies and Gentlemen, it's the moment you have all been waiting for. It's...

AUDIENCE: WHEEL!... OF!... JUSTICE!...

STAGE MANAGER: Yes, Ladies and Gentlemen from our courtroom here at (*your town*), it's North America's most watched game show! (*green light*) The famous wheel is spinning away with an assortment of sentences and fabulous and exciting prizes, from small fines to life imprisonment, just waiting to be won tonight. (*green light*) Now, ladies and gentlemen, here is our host for the evening. Ladies and gentlemen, the trickster from Cree mythology. Some call her Raven, some call her Nanabush, some call her Wadkajunga and Winnebago. Ladies and gentlemen, the trickster, Wīsahkecāhk! (*green light*) Now, ladies and gentlemen, let's let this court session begin!

DEFENCE, PROSECUTION, COURT RECORDER, *and* BAILIFF *enter in single file and begin to dance to rap music.*

JUDGE *enters, hands holding his cloak over his head. Then he drops his cloak and rap-dances with his song.*

JUDGE:

This court's in session
So please all rise

We're going to try to legitimize
Christopher Columbus is the accused
Or is it that he is only confused?
Against him we got litigation
That has something in it concerning our nation
Got exoneration from an allegation
Or will it only be assimilation?
Whatever the case
And it's not yet sealed
But don't you worry
Because here resides... Judge Chesterfield.

DEFENCE, PROSECUTION, COURT RECORDER, and **BAILIFF:** Uh!

Green light. Everyone is seated.

BAILIFF: All rise. Judge Chesterfield presiding.

AUDIENCE *stands.*

JUDGE: You may be seated. First case please.

BAILIFF: People versus Christopher Columbus.

ALL:

Christopher Columbus?
Christopher Columbus?
Christopher Columbus?
Christopher Columbus?

The lights fade out. When they come up, a startled CHRISTOPHER
COLUMBUS *is standing at centre stage. He looks frantically around for
something familiar.*

COLUMBUS: Santa Maria! I'ma lost again!

JUDGE: Take your seat, Mr. Columbus. Please Bailiff. Swear the
accused in.

BAILIFF *escorts* COLUMBUS *to his seat.* WĪSAHKECĀHK *moves forward
from the wheel to inspect him. For the rest of this court scene,*
WĪSAHKECĀHK *moves freely about the stage, invisible to everyone in
the courtroom. She moves objects and paper, including the gavel,*

leaves feathers here and there, and often sits on or under tables watching the trial unfold.

BAILIFF: Raise your right hand.

COLUMBUS: Uh, I take it that this is a court of law?

JUDGE: Yes it is, Mr. Columbus.

COLUMBUS: I take it I am on trial here, huh?

JUDGE: You most certainly are.

COLUMBUS: I take it you are in charge of these precedings, hey?

JUDGE: I am the judge for this case, yes.

COLUMBUS: I knew it as soon as I looked at you. You have that look of intelligence in your eye. You have this air of authority. Under dem robes I can see them rippling muscles, hey. Like Adonis. If I was a woman, I would gladly bear your children.

PROSECUTION: Your Honour, that is bribery.

JUDGE: Sustained.

COLUMBUS: I was just getting warmed up.

JUDGE: Swear the accused in, please.

BAILIFF: Raise your right hand. (COLUMBUS *raises his left hand*)

JUDGE: Your *right* hand, Mister Columbus.

COLUMBUS: I'ma sailor, not a scholar, hey!

BAILIFF: Do you swear…

COLUMBUS: I don't swear. I'ma giving it up for Lent.

BAILIFF: Do you swear to tell the truth and nothing but the truth, so help you God?

COLUMBUS: I swear.

JUDGE: Could we have the facts of the case?

COURT RECORDER: Ladies and gentlemen of the court, Christopher Columbus was born in Italy in 1451. In 1486, he requested the support of the King and Queen of Spain to sail west across the Atlantic Ocean in search of the East

Indies. Bankrupt from war and in desperate need for gold, the Spanish monarchy granted Columbus permission. In August of 1492, he set sail with three ships... the Nina, the Pinta, and the Santa Maria. On October 12, 1492 land was sighted. A small island near Jamaica. Columbus tried to force the Taino Indians to find gold, with very little luck. Ten Taino Indians were kidnapped. Two escaped and six were taken back to Spain. One died in Spain, and three died on the journey home. In 1493, Columbus sailed again, with 17 ships and 1200 men. He continued his search for gold and for the East Indies but failed. Columbus subjected the Taino Indians to theft, slavery, rape, and execution. In 1495 he sent 550 Taino slaves to Spain and gave another 1000 slaves to the colonists. Tainos who did not comply were executed. This is the legacy of Columbus's voyage to this land. (*yellow light*)

JUDGE: Thank you. And what is it that Mr. Columbus is being charged with today? Could we hear the charges, please Bailiff?

BAILIFF: Indecent exploration. (*red light*) Vending without a licence. (*red light*) Breaking immigration laws. (*red light*) And defacing public property. (*red light*)

JUDGE: Thank you. Defence, do you have any opening remarks?

DEFENCE: Your Honour, I would like to speak to my client before I begin.

JUDGE: Feel free.

DEFENCE: Thank you. (DEFENCE ATTORNEY *has a private conference with* COLUMBUS) Mr. Columbus, are you guilty of the charges?

COLUMBUS: No. I'ma being framed.

DEFENCE: Very well. Okay Your Honour. I am ready to start my opening remarks.

JUDGE: Proceed.

DEFENCE: Your Honour, fellow attorney, ladies and gentlemen of the jury. Today I would like to introduce you to a person who has been very famous for five hundred years – Mr. Christopher Columbus. Many history books and TV movies have portrayed him as a villain... as someone who has taken the land of the Americas, but this is not true. My client is innocent! I tell you he is innocent of any charges that have been laid against him. He is an honorable man who has come to this country. The queen asked him to find some new land and he has done this. Look at this face. (DEFENCE *holds his face in both hands*) This innocent face. (COLUMBUS *tries to look pathetic*) Could a face like this hurt anyone? (*red light*)

PROSECUTION: Objection.

JUDGE: Over-ruled. Prosecution, you shall not object during the opening remarks. You may continue.

DEFENCE: Thank you, Your Honour.

COLUMBUS: You are a very fair man, judge.

DEFENCE: Look at this face! A face that any mother could love. Could this face ever be accused of anything? He is innocent. Ladies and gentlemen of the jury, please, I would like you to know that all these charges against my client have been trumped up. He is innocent of all charges and today I will prove it. I will definitely prove it.

COLUMBUS: I'ma being framed! (*red light*)

JUDGE: We will let the court decide on that, Mr. Columbus. Prosecution do you have any opening remarks?

PROSECUTION: Yes, I do Your Honour. Ladies and gentlemen of the jury, Your Honour, defence attorney, today we have before us one of the hardest tasks we will ever face. For over five hundred years this man has poisoned the minds of our children – for generations. The textbooks the defence attorney has referred to have been full of nothing but lies about the greatness of this person. I want you to think back to 1492 when this so-called explorer set foot for the first time on Native land and claimed it for his own. Ask yourselves if someone who dresses like this could be someone you could trust. (*green light*)

DEFENCE: Objection, Your Honour!

COLUMBUS: That is not a my fault. My wife, she dresses me this way. (*red light*)

PROSECUTION: I intend to show today, Your Honour, all the facts that prove Mr. Columbus is guilty! Guilty as charged! This is a simple open and shut case. I urge you all to keep an open mind to the facts presented in this case. Something that has been ignored for the last five hundred years. I have no further remarks. (*green light*)

JUDGE: Could we have some order in this court please?

COLUMBUS: Backa home we have a name for people like you. We call em "the jacka-ass."

JUDGE: That shall be stricken.

COLUMBUS: You can strike it, but they are still going to know it!

JUDGE: Mr. Columbus, that is your first warning.

COLUMBUS: How many do I get?

JUDGE: Consider that two. (*to* DEFENCE) Could you please speak to your client for a moment? The court will not tolerate this type of behaviour.

DEFENCE: Mr. Columbus, in North America you can't use language like that.

COLUMBUS: Okay, but he is starting to tick me off, hey!

JUDGE: Stricken! Would you like to call upon your first witness, please?

DEFENCE: Yes, Your Honour. At this time I would like to call Mr. Columbus as my first witness, please.

JUDGE: Mr. Columbus is seated and has been sworn in.

DEFENCE: Thank you, Your Honour. Now Mr. Columbus, after all these years have passed, I am sure that this doesn't seem like a fair deal to you. Could you explain what your idea of this trial is?

COLUMBUS: I'ma very glad that after five hundred years, you know, that I get a chance to put forth my side of – (*He notices television cameras in the crowd*) What are those things?

JUDGE: Those are cameras, Mr. Columbus.

COLUMBUS: We are on TV?

JUDGE: Yes, if you had listened earlier you would have realized that this is one of the first live recordings of a trial in Canada.

COLUMBUS: Are they on me now?

JUDGE: Yes, Mr. Columbus.

COLUMBUS: Which one?

JUDGE: Both of them.

COLUMBUS: (*turns his head to show his profile*) This is my good side... I would like to say a couple of words in my defence, hey. (COLUMBUS *jumps up and moves to the centre of the stage, shouting*) I'ma being shafted! I come to this country, and they take advantage of me. I am an immigrant to this country, but they take advantage of me.

JUDGE: I would ask the defence attorney that you keep your client under control. This is not a zoo. Bailiff, please escort Mr. Columbus back to his seat.

DEFENCE: I am sorry, Your Honour. My client was not aware of the fact that he had to remain seated while speaking. He was just speaking in his own defence, Your Honour.

JUDGE: Consider the fact that this is not an off-Broadway production but a courtroom. Mr. Columbus that is the third time!

DEFENCE: I believe that you were charged with indecent exploration. Could you explain this charge to me?

COLUMBUS: That is totally false. That is a lie. There is no way she could have seen me. The shades, they wasa drawn. She wasa dark and besides I was awearing my mask. I wasn't there! (*red light*)

DEFENCE: Now, Mr. Columbus. I believe the second charge against you is vending without a license. Is it indeed a fact that you gave your precious jewels away? (*green light. COLUMBUS shifts uncomfortably and crosses his legs*)

COLUMBUS: I wish you would rephrase that. My jewels, as you say, are very precious to me... I like to bring beads. I bringa jewellery. These things theys all handcrafted, I make em myself. You can not put a price tag on these things. They are very valuable. I give these things away, huh? So I don't want to hurt their feelings. What do they give me, huh? Dead animals. (*pulls a stuffed beaver out of his satchel*) What can you do with a dead animal, hey? I didn't want to hurt their feelings so I take them. I am the one being taken advantage of. But I don't get mad. I am a nice guy. (*reaches out and fingers the* JUDGE's *robe*) Is that silk?

JUDGE: No, that is cotton, Mr. Columbus.

COLUMBUS: That is a very *nice* cotton. I tell you what. I will give you a watch for that robe. I tell you what. I give you this watch, this beautiful watch for that. (*shakes the watch vigorously*) If you shake it, it still works.

PROSECUTION: Your Honour, I believe that he is trying to bribe you. I would like that to go down as Exhibit A.

JUDGE: It shall go down as Exhibit A. Thank you prosecution for correcting my behaviour. Mr. Columbus, you should be ashamed of yourself. Trying to bribe me with a watch with no working parts in it!

COLUMBUS: Oh, I'ma sorry. This is the one I traded with the Indians. (*red light*)

JUDGE: Silence. Any further questioning?

PROSECUTION: Yes, Your Honour. I believe the next charge against you is breaking immigration laws and kidnapping. Isn't it the truth that you were offering luxury cruises to people?

COLUMBUS: That is right. I like to picture myself as a travel agent. I give them a chance to see the world. In my country we don't have these restrictions, you can go anywhere you want. (to PROSECUTION) I take you home, you are doing a good job. You make a good slave. It all kind of reminds me of a song. How does it go? Oh, I remember. (COLUMBUS *rushes to the front of the stage and breaks into song*)

Thisa slave she a my slave
She not a your slave
From Santa Del Mingo
To Vancouver Island
This slave she a made just for me

Now this song she is a classic. She has been in the top ten in my country for fifteen years. Your education is not complete unless you learn this song. So I am going a teach you this song. (*addresses* STAGE MANAGER) Can you come here, please? (STAGE MANAGER *steps onto the stage to hold the words to the song*) I would like you to hold this sign if you don't think it is too tough. (STAGE MANAGER *unrolls the sheet, but holds it wrong side up*) Turn it around hey. (STAGE MANAGER *turns around*. COLUMBUS *is disgusted*) Hold it up over your head. (STAGE MANAGER *does*) He is not a very bright, eh? You just can't get good help nowadays. (*He grabs* STAGE MANAGER, *turns him around, and turns the sheet right side up*) Now you repeat after me. I sing a line and then I want you to sing it with feeling and emotion.

COLUMBUS:

This a land she a your land

AUDIENCE:

This a land she is your land

COLUMBUS: What's the matter? The cat, she gotta your tongue? We try again.

This a land she a your land

AUDIENCE:

This a land she a your land

COLUMBUS: There is not a whole bunch of enthusiasm. Let's try it again.

She not our land

AUDIENCE:

She not our land

COLUMBUS:

From the Redwood Forest

AUDIENCE:

From the Redwood Forest

COLUMBUS:

To the Gulf Stream watah

AUDIENCE:

To the Gulf Stream watah

COLUMBUS:

This land she a made just for you…. That'sa me

AUDIENCE:

This land she a made just for you.

STAGE MANAGER:

That's a me.

COLUMBUS: That is my line.

STAGE MANAGER: That is my line.

COLUMBUS: I do it myself. (*yanks sheet from* STAGE MANAGER. STAGE MANAGER *steps offstage again*) All together.

COLUMBUS and AUDIENCE:

This land shea your land
She not our land
From the Redwood forest

To the Gulf Stream watah
This land she a made just for you

(*as* AUDIENCE *sings,* COLUMBUS *is overcome with emotion*) Oh, you are a making me cry!

PROSECUTION: Objection, Your Honour. I would like whatever is going on in this courtroom to stop.

DEFENCE: I am sorry, Your Honour. Once again my client has been overcome by emotion and just reacted. Your Honour, I am sorry.

JUDGE: We shall continue this case. Mr. Columbus, there is something I must say. This is a courtroom, she a my courtroom. She a not your courtroom. Mr. Columbus, you shall be held in contempt.

DEFENCE: In contempt for what Your Honour? He is an innocent immigrant. He did not know any better in doing this.

JUDGE: Mr. Columbus has been warned more than enough. Do you have further questioning?

DEFENCE: Yes, Your Honour. The last charge against my client was defacing public property. Another crude, made-up charge against him. I do not believe that there has been any defacing of public property. Mr. Columbus would you explain that please?

COLUMBUS: That is totally false. When I come to this country it is a wasteland. There is nothing here. I come to this valley and I find this hole.

JUDGE *notices that he is holding a feather. In* COLUMBUS'*s hand is his gavel, thanks to the trickery of* WĪSAHKECĀHK.

JUDGE: Mr. Columbus, is that not my gavel?

COLUMBUS: She is mine now. You got a my watch.

JUDGE: I also have a feather!

DEFENCE: What are you doing with a feather, Your Honour?

JUDGE *snatches back his gavel and bangs it on the desk.*

JUDGE: I have no idea. Continue, Mr. Columbus.

COLUMBUS: She is a wasteland. I come to this meadow, hey? There is this hole and she is just a begging me to plant my flag. I take my flag and I plant my flag. Now she is my land. These people they come onto my land. They are trespassing. I could sue but I don't because I am a nice guy.

PROSECUTION *notices that there is a feather in the hair of the* DEFENCE. WĪSAHKECĀHK *watches all of this, laughing.*

PROSECUTION: What is wrong with the defence attorney?

BAILIFF: *(laughing)* I believe the defence is moulting, Your Honour.

DEFENCE: Objection, Your Honour. The prosecution deliberately put that feather in my hair. As she passed me this morning in the hallway she bumped me.

JUDGE: Bailiff, could you check for birds, please? Let's continue!

DEFENCE: At this time, Your Honour, I have no more questions for my client. I will rest at this time, Your Honour.

JUDGE: Thank you. Prosecution, would you like to cross examine the witness?

PROSECUTION: Yes, Your Honour. Mr. Columbus I would like you to tell the ladies and gentlemen of the jury where you were on September 14, 1492 at approximately 2 PM in the afternoon.

COLUMBUS: September 14th huh?

PROSECUTION: Yes, I believe it was a Friday, sir.

COLUMBUS: 1492 hey?

PROSECUTION: 1492.

COLUMBUS: I was playing racquetball. I win two out of three.

PROSECUTION: Racquetball hey? Let me remind you, Mr. Columbus, that perjury is a very serious offense in this country.

COLUMBUS: How serious?

PROSECUTION: Very serious, Mr. Columbus.

COLUMBUS: Well, let's see. On Wednesday we watch All My Slaves. Thursday, that is bingo day on the ship. Friday, we wasa playing lacrosse. That's right. We wasa playing lacrosse. Me and the boys.

PROSECUTION: You are absolutely sure you were playing lacrosse.

COLUMBUS: That is right. That is what I said.

PROSECUTION: Please let the record show that Mr. Columbus says he was playing lacrosse. On your ship, Mr. Columbus, you eat three decent meals a day. Would you care to explain to the ladies and gentlemen of the jury, what kinds of food you eat on the ship?

COLUMBUS: Well, uh…

PROSECUTION: Let me ask first, Mr. Columbus, if you brought this food from your own land?

COLUMBUS: That's right. Just like Mama used to make. When we get up we have some, like a cocoa eh?

PROSECUTION: Cocoa.

COLUMBUS: That's right. And then for dinner we have a turkey sandwich on a bannock bun. And we throw in a little sweet potato and corn, hey.

PROSECUTION: At this point, ladies and gentlemen of the jury, I would like to refresh your memory of all the food and the games that Mr. Columbus has just made us aware of. Lacrosse, turkey, sweet potato, corn, cocoa…. All of these are gifts from the Native people of the Americas. This man is a fraud! (*green light*)

PROSECUTION: Your Honour, I would like this flag to go down as Exhibit B. Mr. Columbus, this is your flag?

COLUMBUS: That's right. And she is a good likeness of me, no?

PROSECUTION: I would like you to explain to the ladies and gentlemen of the jury where exactly you planted this flag.

COLUMBUS: Like I said before… (*to* DEFENCE) She wasn't listening.

DEFENCE: No, she never does.

COLUMBUS: I see this hole. She is just a begging me to plant my flag. So I plant my flag. She is now my land.

PROSECUTION: And there was absolutely no one else around when you planted this flag and claimed this land for your own?

COLUMBUS: No, there was no pepple.

PROSECUTION: No people at all?

COLUMBUS: I don't recall no pepple. (*red light*)

PROSECUTION: No one at all?

COLUMBUS: Well, there were some crechers.

PROSECUTION: Would you care to explain "crechers"?

COLUMBUS: Well, these crechers, they weren't very nice, hey? Here I am a standing there with my flag, and they start throwing these little white eggs at me. And these crechers they's a not very bright. They's a screaming "Fore" and there is only one of me!

PROSECUTION: Mr. Columbus, I believe that you planted your flag on a golf course. And if you planted your flag on a golf course, then it obviously means that it was owned by people before you got there. (*green light*)

COLUMBUS: What is this golf?

PROSECUTION: It is a game.... You have a club.... It is fantastic. You get out, relax. (*mimes the action of swinging a golf club*) There is green for as far as you can see. (*catches herself*) Why am I explaining this to you?

COLUMBUS: I don't know but she sounds like fun. Me and the boys, we got nothing to do on Saturday. Maybe we could play this golf.... Imagine, I just discovered golf! (*red light*)

PROSECUTION: I have one final item here. (*reaches into briefcase for a paper*) I believe, Mr. Columbus... (*pulls out a feather and stares at it*) I find something awfully stupid going on in here. I have to believe that it is the defence attorney that is … (*a shouting match erupts between* DEFENCE *and* PROSECUTION)

DEFENCE: Your Honour, it is obviously this person who has been bringing feathers into the courtroom and making a farce of this whole issue.

PROSECUTION: You really know that you are not going to win, don't you, so you have to add –

DEFENCE: Your Honour, the prosecution obviously has the feathers in her head.

PROSECUTION: I would like to proceed with this case!

JUDGE: Mr. Columbus.

PROSECUTION: I have another exhibit, Your Honour. I believe Mr. Columbus stated in his opening statement that he brought precious jewels from his homeland which he crafted himself. I would like you at this time, Your Honour, to read to the ladies and gentlemen of the jury the inscription of where one of his jewels was made. (*hands a watch to the* JUDGE)

JUDGE: It says "Made in Japan."

PROSECUTION: Made in Japan.… Mr. Columbus, I do not believe that you are an Asian person. Is your homeland Japan?

COLUMBUS: No.

PROSECUTION: Could you explain how one of your handcrafted jewels happens to be made in Japan?

COLUMBUS: (*He fidgets guiltily, caught in the act*) How much time I got? (*long, long pause*) Okay, we took a left where we should have taken a right and we end up in Japan! We make it on the ship at Japan! … She still a handcrafted! (*red light*)

PROSECUTION: Your Honour, this person is a fraud and I have no more questions for him.

JUDGE: Do you have another witness you would like to call upon, defence?

DEFENCE: Yes, at this time I would like to call three specific witnesses that have worked with Mr. Columbus for a long time. The three character witnesses I would like to call are the Nina, Pinta, and Santa Maria.

Music and flashing lights. The green light flashes repeatedly. NINA, PINTA, SANTA MARIA *whoop and dance their way on stage.*

PROSECUTION: Objection, Your Honour!

JUDGE: Sit down counsellor. A little entertainment never hurt anyone.

The three ships line up at centre stage, facing the audience.

NINA: Ladies and gentlemen, we are just so thrilled to be here. We are honoured to be here to testify about… about Christopher's prowess as a… a… sailor! *(all three laugh)* You know, when Christopher asked us if we wanted to go for a great *sail*… well, we said we'd go anywhere for a bargain! *(they laugh)*

PINTA: But when Christopher said we were going across the ocean, we said, "Oh no, Christopher. We'd *rudder* not! We couldn't *fathom* doing that! *(they laugh)* That's out of our *league*!"

SANTA MARIA: But you know Christopher! When he said "All hands on deck," well… you just obeyed. *(they laugh)* "You'd better shape up and ship out," he said. Then he rigged our sails, raised our anchors, and off we went. Christopher never was one to *harbour* a grudge.

NINA: And now, ladies and gentlemen, we would like to sing a song that we wrote just for you. Are you ready? One, two, three, hit it.

ALL THREE:

Take us out on the ocean
Take us out for a ride
Give us some cultures that we can attack
Give us some slaves that we can take back
Cause it's hip, hip, hip for Columbus
If he don't get gold it's a shame
For it's Nina, Pinta, and Santa Maria in the New Found Land

Music. Flashing lights. All three traffic lights flash on – red, green, and yellow. NINA, PINTA, *and* SANTA MARIA *dance off. The* PROSECUTION *is yelling in the midst of this mayhem.*

PROSECUTION: I object to this demonstration, Your Honour!

DEFENCE: Objection, Your Honour. I'll have you know that these are three very good character witnesses. They worked for Mr. Columbus for a very long, long, long, long, long time.

JUDGE: Counsellors, sit down. Your objection to her objection is sustained. Your objection is overruled. The court will recognize those three character witnesses as… three of the most legitimate witnesses I think we have ever seen. (*red light*) We shall carry on. Do you have any further witnesses you would like to call upon, defence?

DEFENCE: No. Your Honour. I think I have proven that all these charges against my client have been trumped up. He is innocent of all the charges. He is innocent and I am sure the jury will find him that way. Thank you, Your Honour.

JUDGE: Defence rests. Prosecution, you may call upon your witnesses please.

PROSECUTION: Your Honour. (*long pause*) We have only the voices from the past.

Indian flute music. Lights fade to black. VOICES *speak from the darkness, from around the* AUDIENCE.

VOICE ONE: I am a Taino woman. My people lived on the island of Bohio. One day Columbus appeared and acted as if the land belonged to him. My people thought this odd, for we do not believe that land is something that we own. Besides, we were already living there. Columbus made it clear that he wanted gold. If my people did not bring him gold, he had their hands cut off. Many of my people bled to death. We tried to form an army, but because we did not have the guns, the swords, or the vicious dogs used by Columbus and his men, we were defeated. My people were forced to run for their lives. Those that were captured were hung or burned to death. Many of my people killed themselves. Before long almost all of the Taino were killed. Other Aboriginals in the Americas were attacked, some with weapons and some with terrible new diseases. But not all have been destroyed. Some have survived. We have little left to show our children, but we have our story. A story told from generation to generation. Stories that tell of the cruel genocide of my people.

Red light on centre stage. WĪSAHKECĀHK *dances slowly to the flute music. Red light and music, then fade.*

VOICE TWO: I am Chief Dan George. I have always tried to teach my people that man and creatures must try to walk together as one. Will our brothers the salmon always find a place to spawn? Will the bear cubs always have a tree to climb? There is little time left and much effort needed. Will the eagle continue to soar in freedom? All I can do is hope.

Red light on. WĪSAHKECĀHK *dancing. Then fade.*

VOICE THREE: Listen to the winds of time. It echoes the words of promises. Promises of treaties and a new beginning. Sign a treaty with the great white mother and the following shall come to pass. What I offer does not take away your way of life. You will have then as you have now. As long as the sun shines, the grass grows and the river flows.

Red light on. WĪSAHKECĀHK *dancing. Then fade.*

VOICE FOUR: I am an Aboriginal woman, stripped of my status and culture and left with no identity because I married someone non-Aboriginal. In the time prior to contact I was a respected part of my people's existence. Since contact I have slowly been removed from my place of Honour in our society. I have had to fight hard to survive and for education and other rights denied me. Through Bill C31, I have finally redeemed my birthright and my children and I can return to our roots and watch the land become whole.

Red light on. WĪSAHKECĀHK *dancing. Then fade.*

VOICE FIVE: I am a white woman rereading history. It is estimated that when Columbus arrived in North America there were some twenty-five million people living here.

Some estimates go as high as sixty million. But it wasn't Columbus's guns or the cruelty of the men that came later with their guns, swords, and vicious dogs. It was the diseases that they brought with them. Sixty new diseases. Smallpox, diptheria, typhoid. By the end of the century the population of the Americas was under one million. It gives new meaning to the words "conquest," "discovery," "assimilation."

Red light on. WĪSAHKECĀHK dancing. Then fade.

VOICE SIX: You do not know me because I am not a famous person, but you have met me or someone just like me. I represent many different women. I dropped out of school at a young age. Boredom and peer pressure introduced me to the drug and alcohol scene. Still just a child myself, I became a mother, young, inexperienced and unwed. With hardly any parenting skills, I tried to look after my baby but I couldn't seem to cope with all the responsibilities. Employers would not hire me because of the colour of my skin and no work experience. I couldn't get any help from welfare because I was physically able to work. I was desperate so I started to steal to support my baby and eventually I was caught and charged. I was an innocent victim of a vicious cycle. I spent many years in and out of the justice and welfare systems. Because no one cared to look past the colour of my skin.

Red light on. WĪSAHKECĀHK dancing. Then fade.

VOICE SEVEN: My name is Louis David Riel. I am a condemned man. But at least I have been proven not to be a fool. That will be a conciliation for my mother, my wife, and my children, for my country, for my people. I have helped to build a new nation of people, a Métis nation. And for that I will be forever proud. No man or court can ever take that away from me. Whatever you do to me, I hope you do something to console those who have partaken only of my sufferings. It will be rendered back to you a hundred times in this world and in the next. My prayers go with my people. May God provide for them and make them strong. We have no shame for what we have done. Only pride. Your Honours, that is what I have to say.

Red light on. WĪSAHKECĀHK *dancing. Then light and music fade to darkness and silence. A long pause.*

PROSECUTION: Your Honour, the prosecution rests.

JUDGE: *(gavel pounds)* Ladies and gentlemen. The court has arrived at a decision. Could we have the verdict, please?

A pause, then the wheel starts to spin. As it clicks faster and faster, voices call the verdict from the darkness, and all of the actors move quietly onto the stage. They form a semi-circle behind WĪSAHKECĀHK.

VOICES: Guilty. Guilty. Guilty. Guilty. Guilty. Guilty. Guilty. Guilty.

The light slowly rises and the AUDIENCE *sees the wheel spinning.* WĪSAHKECĀHK *faces it and moves her arms as if she is magically spin-spinning it from a distance. As she moves slower and slower, the wheel spins slower and slower. It goes past the "guilty" verdict, stops, then mysteriously turns back to ... "guilty."* WĪSAHKECĀHK *turns slowly, a feather in each hand. She raises them high and speaks for the first time. She speaks in Cree, a Cree prayer. As she lowers the feathers, powwow music begins to rise. She dances, slowly at first, then with more and more spirit as the music builds. She is celebrating.*

END

Switching Places

Rex Deverell

I REMEMBER THE GENESIS OF THIS play very well. The voice on the phone said, "You don't know me but I'm a social worker and I have a group of teenage mothers who want to tell their stories."

That call led me to become a regular attender in a self-help group for young (mostly single) mothers (or mothers-to-be)! It was an education. These women were growing up in a hurry. They talked (often with wry humour) about how hard it was to survive, to make a life for themselves and their babies. But they also wept when they spoke of the rifts which had been caused by their pregnancy. Some had been rejected by their parents, some had lost friends. Career and educational goals had been put on hold. The party girl could no longer party. Welfare was not all that much fun for those who were on it. They spoke of their feelings towards the fathers of their children. Sometimes these boys were trying to help but more often the pregnancy had put an end to the relationship. They also spoke of moments when their despair and frustration would erupt into anger at their babies. They talked of how frightened they were of becoming violent and abusive. At one of the meetings someone said, "If boys had to go through all this, I bet they'd have better attitudes." I thought – well, why not? It's going to be a play. In plays things can happen that in real life we can only wish for. The result was *Switching Places*.

So I want to thank that anonymous group of single mothers. They helped me give birth to an instructive and, I think, entertaining new play. Through the Globe Theatre school tour and now this published edition they have done what they set out to do – they have shared their stories.

Rex Deverell is alive and well and living in the woods somewhere in Ontario. From 1975 to 1990 he was the award-winning playwright-in-residence at the Globe Theatre in Regina. He is married to broadcaster Rita Deverell, and they have a son, Ramsay. Rex continues to write plays and a recent one, "The Short Circuit," for secondary school audiences, has received a Chalmers Award nomination.

Switching Places was produced by the Globe Theatre's touring company in the fall of 1986 and spring of 1987. The cast was:

MACHOGOD . . . . Dennis Fitzgerald
SCOTT . . . . Birk Lawrence
SAL . . . . Christina Nicoll
SEXGODDESS . . . . Jennifer Nokes
DIRECTOR . . . . Brian Way
STAGE MANAGER . . . . Jean Southgate
DESIGNER. . . . . Jo Dibb

Characters

MACHOGOD: *Machismo personified. He will step into other roles when required by the story.*

SEXGODDESS: *Venus with an attitude. She will step into other roles when required by the story.*

SAL: *A teenager. A glowing, self-possessed girl.*

SCOTT: *A teenager. Has always considered himself to be God's gift to women.*

Set Description

The playing area is set with four tall stools. The original production was staged in the round with very little in the way of sets. The actors pantomimed props except where indicated in the script – e.g., a real baby's rattle. When the gods step into human roles, they may put on a hat or use an actual prop to help identify their new character.

Scene One

Four figures enter the area from four directions. They stand passively, surveying the audience. Two of these are the SEX GODS – MACHOGOD *and* SEXGODDESS. *The other two are teenagers –* SAL *and* SCOTT. *The* GODS *complete their inspection of the audience and* SEXGODDESS *nods to the others. All sit down except for* SCOTT, *who addresses the audience.*

SCOTT: Normally I don't talk about sex in front of an audience. But I have this agreement, see: I have to tell you exactly what happened. *(pause and then a little more cockily)* In fact, normally I don't talk about sex at all. I just do it. I'm an action man not a – *(SEX GODS rise)* Sorry. Sorry. *(to the audience)* I've got this agreement – *(to the GODS)* I'm telling them. *(the SEX GODS sit down. To the audience)* This all started the time the Sex Gods came together for their professional development day. They were meeting at the Holiday Inn. *(breaks off)* The Sex Gods. Don't you know about the Sex Gods? Yeah, there are such things. Believe me. Anyway these Sex Gods were all registering at the registration table and then being shunted off for coffee and stale donuts before the first workshop – when one of them saw someone she hadn't seen for ages…

SEXGODDESS: MachoGod!

MACHOGOD: Hey, what's happenin', Babe!

SEXGODDESS: I haven't seen you for ages. And don't call me babe. Where you been, man?

MACHOGOD: Around, if you know what I mean.

SEXGODDESS: You old devil, why don't you spell it out for me?

MACHOGOD: You don't want to hear. It would burn your ears.

SEXGODDESS: Try me.

MACHOGOD: *(wolfish)* I'd like to, babe…

SEXGODDESS: Watchit…

MACHOGOD: *(backing off)* But being aware of your formidable powers as a goddess –

SEXGODDESS: – and having a strong concern for your health and wellbeing…

MACHOGOD: I shall remain at a respectful distance.

SEXGODDESS: I do like you, MachoGod – but a respectful distance is where I like you best.

MACHOGOD: Hokay.

SEXGODDESS: Hokay. So spell it out for me.

MACHOGOD: Hey! The adolescent beat.

SEXGODDESS: (alarmed) Oh oh.

MACHOGOD: Oh yes, my favourite assignment –

SEXGODDESS: Kids…

MACHOGOD: Young men and young women!

SEXGODDESS: Don't they have enough to worry about…

MACHOGOD: Love 'em! All those hormones, all those gonads, all those genes bursting their seams…

SEXGODDESS: You are trouble, Macho –…

MACHOGOD: And me – prowling through the halls of education peeking in the lockers, examining the graffiti in the washrooms, giving a few pointers to the guys – if you know what I mean.…

SEXGODDESS: Jock training.

MACHOGOD: In short, I've been in heaven! How about you?

SEXGODDESS: Not snooping into people's lockers, that's for sure. Let me tell you, man. I've been having the greatest time! I have been dancing at the top of the charts. I have been on the women's shift –

MACHOGOD: (snorting) The women's shift. And how are the little ladies –

SEXGODDESS: Move off. The little ladies are just fine, thank you. How are all your little gentlemen?

MACHOGOD: *(scornfully)* Gentlemen? Oh, don't you wish! Drop the gentle, okay? Just drop it. What we are talking about here is *men*!

SEXGODDESS: Cavemen.

MACHOGOD: Yeah, if you like. There was a lot to be said for the cavemen. I liked it in those days....

SEXGODDESS: Conking women with clubs, dragging them off by their hair....

MACHOGOD: *(blissful)* Ah yes, those were the days... simpler times, Goddess, simpler and happier times. Now look at what a guy has to put up with – look at the hoops a guy has to jump through – just to get a little warmth and female affection. You have to worry about AIDS. Sometimes you even have to pretend women should have equality. Let me tell you, times are tough. Times are tough.

SEXGODDESS: *(sarcastic)* I'm so sympathetic.

MACHOGOD: But still, I've got some promising youngsters coming up. Have you considered my man, Scott?

SEXGODDESS: Who?

MACHOGOD: Scott idol-of-the-Saturday-night-set Staples. Let me point him out to you.

SEXGODDESS: Point him out to me.

SCOTT *rises and begins to lift weights.*

SCOTT: Scott – *(meaningfully)* with two T's.

MACHOGOD: That's my man. Believe me – there's somebody who has studied the arts of manliness –

SEXGODDESS: With who – King Kong?

MACHOGOD: With me, of course. He doesn't realize the source of his expertise – but he's got it, nevertheless – *(chanting to himself and snapping his fingers)* He's got it, he's got it! Oh yes indeed he's got it.

SEXGODDESS: Got what? Athlete's foot?

MACHOGOD: Don't put him down, Goddess. This kid has got what it takes.

SEXGODDESS: And what does it take?

MACHOGOD: Charm, *savoir faire*, looks, animal magnetism, nerve, verve, flair! I wrote the book and he learned it off by heart.

SEXGODDESS: Did he?

MACHOGOD: He did. He has all the right attitudes. Sow your wild oats while ye may. Love 'em and leave 'em. Never get too involved. Keep all your options open. Never say I love you – except as a last resort. All the right attitudes. Girls are putty in his fingers.

SEXGODDESS: Are they?

MACHOGOD: Would you like to make a small wager?

SEXGODDESS: Are you telling me some girl is dumb enough to fall for all that tired old stuff?

MACHOGOD: Dumb is not the question, Goddess. Women can get very wily. But if a man's on his toes and he plays his cards right – they always fall.

SEXGODDESS: Always?

MACHOGOD: Always. How about it, Goddess? Are you going to take the bet or not?

SEXGODDESS: What kind of a bet?

MACHOGOD: See that girl?

SEXGODDESS: Yeah.

MACHOGOD: Let's say – if Scott Staples can't hit a home run with that girl, I shall put up a small notice on Mount Olympus admitting in all humility that you are the stronger sex.

SEXGODDESS: And if he can?

MACHOGOD: I take over the world.

SEXGODDESS: How about a short vacation on Malibu?

MACHOGOD: Done.

SEXGODDESS: Coaching illegal.

MACHOGOD: Right.

SEXGODDESS: For both of us.

MACHOGOD: Sure.

SEXGODDESS: Okay, MachoGod. Strut your stuff.

MACHOGOD: Right – may I present The Victim, I mean The Broad – I mean this lovely young example of feminine pulchritude.

SAL *has been watching* SCOTT *show off. The* GODS *back off and she now rises.*

SCOTT: Hi.

SAL: Hello.

SCOTT: Do you pump iron?

SAL: I beg your pardon?

SCOTT: Are you interested in weights?

SAL: Not really.

SEXGODDESS: (*to* MACHOGOD) Putty in his hands.

MACHOGOD: Wait.

SCOTT: You don't do anything like this?

SAL: No.

SCOTT: I don't get it.

SAL: What?

SCOTT: How you could have such a great bod.

MACHOGOD: Oooeee!

SEXGODDESS: She's not going to fall for that.

SAL: That's a line. That is – that is a line.

SEXGODDESS: See?

SAL: But actually I like it.

102

MACHOGOD: See?

SCOTT: Hey.

The two of them smile at each other warmly.

MACHOGOD: Now watch this.

SCOTT: (*suddenly bashful*) Well, uh – I guess – I guess I gotta go. (*long pause.* SAL *shrugs*) Yeah.

He starts to leave.

SAL: Wait.

SCOTT: Yeah?

SAL: What's your name?

SCOTT: Scott.

SAL: Scott?

SCOTT: With two T's. What's yours?

SAL: Sally. But don't call me that. Call me Sal.

SCOTT: Sure thing. See you around, Sal.

SAL: Sure.

SCOTT *exits.* SAL *takes a moment and exits.*

MACHOGOD: First base.

SEXGODDESS: Cute.

MACHOGOD: Lesson number one. Make the most of what you've got – if muscles don't work, try shy and sensitive.

SEXGODDESS: Maybe the guy is shy and sensitive.

MACHOGOD: (*sincerely*) Maybe he is. You've gotta give him the benefit of the doubt, eh?

SEXGODDESS: Why not?

MACHOGOD: (*slapping his knee*) First base! Now watch the next move.

SCOTT: (*entering, as if in a store*) What do I have to do to get served here?

MACHOGOD: You'll have to help out.

SEXGODDESS: Not on your life.

MACHOGOD: Cold feet?

SEXGODDESS *assumes the character of a store clerk.*

SEXGODDESS: *(to* SCOTT*)* May I help you, young man?

SCOTT: I'm not sure. Do you have something for a girl?

SEXGODDESS: What kind of girl?

SCOTT: You know, just a girl.

SEXGODDESS: How old?

SCOTT: My age, maybe.

SEXGODDESS: What does she like?

SCOTT: I don't know – whatever girls like, I guess.

SEXGODDESS: Every girl is different.

SCOTT: Not deep down.

SEXGODDESS: I see.

SCOTT: Have you got flowers?

SEXGODDESS: A small selection.

SCOTT: Okay, give me some flowers.

SEXGODDESS: Any particular flowers?

SCOTT: Whatever you think a girl would like. As long as they
don't cost over – *(consults his wallet)* three-fifty.

SEXGODDESS: *(wryly)* Come this way.

Resuming character she crosses to the MACHOGOD. SCOTT *starts after
her but* SAL *appears with a bouquet of flowers.*

SAL: Oh, Scott! *(he stops and then assumes his bashful nice guy
character)* How did you know I liked flowers?

SCOTT: I didn't...

SEXGODDESS: *(aside)* Neither did I.

SCOTT: Do you really?

SAL: What?

SCOTT: Like them?

SAL: It's corny but it's nice.

SCOTT: Sally? – I mean – Sal?

SAL: Yeah?

SCOTT: You want to go to the show tonight?

SAL: Might be fun. What's on?

SCOTT: Well, downtown there's "Wayne's World 15: Wayne's Revenge" ... and at the drive-in ...

MACHOGOD: Go for broke, my boy ...

SEXGODDESS: (to MACHOGOD) You're disgusting, you know.

SCOTT: It's "I Was a Teenage Mud Wrestler" – I don't know what it's about actually –

SEXGODDESS: I'll bet.

SCOTT: So let's go and see "Wayne's Revenge."

SEXGODDESS: What?

MACHOGOD: Oh no.

SAL: I've seen it already –

SCOTT: So have I.

SAL: Really?

SCOTT: Really. When did you see it?

SAL: Last Friday.

SCOTT: You're kidding(!)?

SAL: No, really.

SCOTT: That's when I was there. I coulda been sitting right behind you!

SAL: That's beyond the cosmos, right?

SCOTT: Right.

SAL: I didn't even see you.

SCOTT: You didn't even know me.

SAL: Fantastic.

They laugh.

SCOTT: Do you want to see it again? (*She shakes her head*) Me neither. So that leaves us with –

SAL: The drive-in.

SCOTT: We could split if we don't like the movie.

SAL: Sure.

SCOTT: Pick you up at nine.

SAL: See yah!

Exit.

MACHOGOD: Hah, second base! Had me worried there for a second but my man came through in the end.

SEXGODDESS: He knew she'd seen that movie. He was sitting right behind her. I'm beginning to think this girl is dumb.

MACHOGOD: Dumb? No, this girl is smart. But my man Scott is smarter. Watch this.

Sound of car pulling up. Enter SCOTT *and* SAL.

SAL: That was fun.

SCOTT: The movie?

SAL: No…

SCOTT: Because I thought it was kind of gross.

SAL: All those gorgeous mud wrestlers?

SCOTT: I couldn't keep my eyes off you.

Long pause.

SAL: I guess I'd better go in.

SCOTT: (*stopping her*) Sally…

SAL: (*hoping he will understand*) I'm old fashioned. (SCOTT *hesitates*) Never kiss first time out.

SCOTT: Oh.

SEXGODDESS: They didn't do anything!

SCOTT: I guess that means...

SEXGODDESS: I win the bet!

MACHOGOD: Not so fast.

SAL: What?

SCOTT: How about the second time?

SAL: You've got a lot of nerve, haven't you?

SCOTT: Tomorrow at eight?

SAL: Sure.

SEXGODDESS: (*turning away*) Oh yuck.

MACHOGOD: Come on, now. You have to admire a guy with so much (*searching for the* mot juste) flair... verve... (*reverently*) moxy.

SCOTT *and* SAL *sit on two stools, side by side.* SCOTT *has his arm around her shoulders. He puts his hand on her knee. She pushes it away. Long pause.*

SCOTT: What's wrong?

SAL: Nothing.

SCOTT: Sure. A week. I can't believe it. Don't you care for me?

SAL: A week?

SCOTT: Yeah. Seven days.

SAL: I don't believe it.

SCOTT: This is like our anniversary, Sal. We started going together a week ago tonight.

SAL: You're so romantic.

SCOTT: So what gives?

SAL: Nothing.

SCOTT: Right, nothing. I'm just somebody to go out with – right?

SAL: Hardly. Hey, lighten up, Scott. I care for you –

SCOTT: Do you?

SAL: A lot.

SCOTT: You don't show it.

SAL: What!? You're crazy. We've gone out a buncha times. We've seen each other practically every chance. You think I'd do that if I didn't like you? My parents are gonna charge you rent – you're here so much.

SCOTT: And so are they.

SAL: Not tonight.

SCOTT: But that's just it. You're acting like your dad's gonna poke his nose in any second.

SAL: Scott.

SCOTT: You are. We're never alone. Even when we're alone.

SAL: What about last night, up on Ripley's Road?

SCOTT: That was nothing. Ripley's believe it or not. Mighty Scott struck out.

SAL: Nothing. What do you call this hickey? I had to wear a turtleneck to school today. You call that nothing?

SCOTT: You know what I mean. (*rising*) Is there something wrong with you?

SEXGODDESS: Oh oh.

MACHOGOD: You have to know when to fire the heavy cannons.

SEXGODDESS: And run up the skull and crossbones.

SAL: Wrong with me? What is that supposed to mean?

SCOTT: Nothing.

SAL: No, tell me.

SCOTT: Forget it.

SAL: Tell me.

SCOTT: I mean sometimes you act like you don't, you know, want it.

SAL: I do not.

SCOTT: I mean we can be really flying, Sal – and then you just go all cold – You're not frigid or anything?

SAL: No!

SCOTT: Don't tell me you're a virgin.

SAL: (*acutely embarrassed*) A virgin? Oh – uh – What makes you think that?

SCOTT: I mean I wouldn't respect you any less or anything. But if that's the problem... I mean... you should tell me.

SAL: It's just that – I guess it's hard to explain.

SCOTT: (*pause*) Does the human body turn you off – like do you think sex is disgusting...

SAL: Come on, I like all that physical stuff –

SCOTT: It's beautiful – it's natural...

SAL: Sure it is. It's just that I don't think I'm ready. I'm sorry, Scott...

SCOTT: You're not religious or anything?

SAL: I'm all kinds of stuff. Will you lighten up.

SCOTT: Is it me? I turn you off, don't I?

SAL: No.

SCOTT: Well then? (*no reply*) Look, a relationship has to go somewhere – or it gets to be a drag. I mean we have to make some kind of progress, right?

SAL: Why are you putting all this pressure on me?

SCOTT: I'm not putting any pressure on you.

SEXGODDESS: Oh yeah?

SCOTT: I'm just trying to figure out why you're putting so much pressure on yourself.

SAL: I like you a lot, Scott. I told you. You don't turn me off. Not at all.

SCOTT: Then what are we waiting for? Hey, we've got a good thing going here. You don't want to break it up, do you?

SAL: No.

SCOTT: Then come on. (*leading her off*) Don't worry. I'll take care of you. It'll be great. Don't worry.

SAL: Scott...

SCOTT: Trust me.

They embrace and freeze.

MACHOGOD: Home run.

SEXGODDESS: You were right.

MACHOGOD: Malibu here I come. (*singing and riding an imaginary wave*) Surfing U.S.A....

SEXGODDESS: (*slyly*) Want some travelling money?

MACHOGOD: (*suspicious*) How do you mean?

SEXGODDESS: Oh, just another little bet...

MACHOGOD: Name it.

SEXGODDESS: That she gets the last laugh.

MACHOGOD: On my man Scott? No way.

SEXGODDESS: Double or nothing.

MACHOGOD: This is like stealing candy from babies. You're on.

SCOTT: (*to audience*) Of course I didn't know what was happening behind the scenes, did I? I didn't even know there was any behind the scenes. Would I have done it any different if I'd known the gods were throwing me like a pair of dice? Probably not.

MACHOGOD: (*taking on the role of a school crony*) Hey, Scott!

SCOTT: What do you say!

Intricate handshake.

MACHOGOD: So tell me!

SCOTT: *(playing innocent)* Tell you what?

MACHOGOD: Come on, Scott. You know what.

SCOTT: I give up.

MACHOGOD: The action, man. How was the action?

SCOTT: When?

MACHOGOD: When? Last Christmas. No, you zit head! Last night.

SCOTT: Oh that.

MACHOGOD: So how about it? Did you get lucky?

SCOTT: *(lets the suspense build for a moment and then)* Of course.

MACHOGOD: *(awestruck)* You lucky dog. I never thought she'd be that easy.

SCOTT: Like stealing candy from a baby.

MACHOGOD: Really? *(casually)* So are you and Sal going together now?

SCOTT: Why?

MACHOGOD: No reason.

SCOTT: You like her, don'tcha?

MACHOGOD: Well…

SCOTT: You like her!

MACHOGOD: I just wondered if you… I mean, if she…

SCOTT: You know me. Be my guest.

MACHOGOD: Alriiiight! *(pause)* Did you use a condom or anything?

SCOTT: What's it to you?

MACHOGOD: If I catch some disease I'll know where it came from.

SCOTT: I'm clean.

MACHOGOD: But did you wear one?

SCOTT: Spoils the fun.

MACHOGOD: Yeah, right. So she's on the pill, eh?

SCOTT: Who cares? That's her problem. I'm not the one that gets pregnant.

SEXGODDESS: Wanna bet?

She snaps her fingers.

SCOTT: Ow.

MACHOGOD: What's wrong?

SCOTT: I don't know – just hurt for a second.

MACHOGOD: Like what?

SEXGODDESS: Like revenge.

MACHOGOD *reverts to himself.*

MACHOGOD: (*to* SEXGODDESS) What did you do?

SEXGODDESS: Wait and see.

Meanwhile SAL *is dialing phone. Phone rings.* GODDESS *picks it up.*

SEXGODDESS: Hello?

SAL: (*uncertain of herself*) Hello, Mrs. Staples?

SEXGODDESS: (*becoming* SCOTT's *mother*) Yes?

SAL: Is Scott in?

SEXGODDESS: Just a second – (*calling*) Scott, it's for you! (*into the phone*) Just a second.

SCOTT: Who is it?

SEXGODDESS: How should I know?

SCOTT: Male or female?

SEXGODDESS: Yes.

SCOTT: Is it Sally or Renata?

SEXGODDESS: I'm not your social secretary. Come down here. Talk to her yourself.

SCOTT: If it's Sally – I don't want to talk to her...

SEXGODDESS: I don't know if it's Sally.

SCOTT: Well, ask her.

SEXGODDESS: I will not.

SCOTT: Say I'm not home.

SEXGODDESS: *(into the phone)* He'll be down in a second. (GODDESS *goes and drags* SCOTT *towards the phone*) Get that phone and then get back up here and clean up your room!

SCOTT: *(into phone)* Hello?

SAL: Scott.

SCOTT: Oh. Hello, Sal.

Glares at mother. The SEXGODDESS *shrugs.*

SAL: Do you want to meet me after school?

SCOTT: Sure. Oh heck. I forgot, I've got a basketball practice.

SAL: I could stick around for that.

SCOTT: Uh, I don't think that's a good idea because I don't know when we'll get out exactly or anything and after that, like I have to be home early, you know what I mean?

SAL: Yeah.

SCOTT: Yeah. Well, I gotta go.

SAL: Scott?

SCOTT: Gotta go, Sal.

SAL: Scott.

SCOTT: Make it quick.

SAL: Is this about last night?

SCOTT: Hey, last night was great, Babe...

SAL: I thought it was...

SCOTT: Right!

SAL: So what's wrong now?

SCOTT: Nothing. I'll see ya, okay?

SAL: When?

SCOTT: I'm not sure. Soon as I get a minute, okay?

SAL: Sure.

Pause.

SCOTT: Gotta go. (*He hangs up*)

SAL: Okay.

SAL *hangs up the phone. The* SEXGODDESS *crosses behind her and puts comforting hands on her shoulders.*

SEXGODDESS: (*to* SCOTT) Just wait in there, young man. The doctor will be with you in a minute.

SCOTT: (*mumbling*) Thanks. Okay. (SCOTT *looks around the doctor's dispensary, grimacing at the anatomical charts*) I hate the artwork.

MACHOGOD: (*breezing in as doctor*) Hello, Scott.

SCOTT: (*unenthusiastic*) Hi.

MACHOGOD: What seems to be the trouble, Scott?

SCOTT: I've been barfing my guts up.

MACHOGOD: I see. (*writing in file*) Severe nausea. There's a lot of flu going around.

SCOTT: You think that's it?

MACHOGOD: Maybe. (*stethoscope*) Breathe in. Out. Again. Again. How long has this been going on?

SCOTT: A couple of weeks.

MACHOGOD: Mmmm.

SCOTT: Funny thing, though.

MACHOGOD: What's that?

SCOTT: I'm always hungry.

MACHOGOD: If you were a girl, I'd give you a pregnancy test, hah hah.

SCOTT: Hahahahahah.

SEXGODDESS: Hahahahahah.

SCOTT: Did you hear something?

MACHOGOD: No.

SCOTT: I thought I heard someone laughing.

MACHOGOD: (*tongue depressor*) Say ah. Strange.

SCOTT: What?

Eyes, ears.

MACHOGOD: Oh, nothing. Don't worry. We'll run a few tests: X-rays, blood, the works. Don't worry. We'll find it. It's probably something simple. (*turns to* GODDESS) You didn't.

SEXGODDESS: Yes I did.

MACHOGOD: That's cheating. (*to* SCOTT) You can button up your shirt.

SEXGODDESS: Lesson number one. Make the most of what you've got.

MACHOGOD: Using divine power is against the rules.

SEXGODDESS: Whose rules? You'd better get back to your patient, Doctor.

MACHOGOD: (*to* SCOTT) Scott! Well, well, well, well. (*pause*) How are you today?

SCOTT: Isn't that what you're supposed to tell me?

MACHOGOD: Yes – hmmm.

SCOTT: You got the results from the tests.

MACHOGOD: Maybe you'd better sit down, Scott.

SCOTT: How long have I got to live?

MACHOGOD: Oh, it's not that bad. You'll live to be an old – uh – man.

SCOTT: *(relieved)* So what's wrong?

MACHOGOD: Scott, you're pregnant.

SCOTT: Is that possible?

MACHOGOD: No.

SCOTT: Heheheh. So what's wrong?

MACHOGOD: You're pregnant. Listen – would you mind checking into the hospital for a few days? We'd like to run a few more tests. I'd like to introduce you to some of my colleagues, perhaps take you to a medical convention –

SCOTT: What?

MACHOGOD: Well, I'm – I mean *you* are making scientific history here.

SCOTT: Forget it.

MACHOGOD: But you owe it to medical science!

SCOTT: Why don't you sell me to the circus?

MACHOGOD: Do you think I could? Just kidding.

SCOTT: Leave me alone.

MACHOGOD: You have to co-operate. This could make my career!

SCOTT: I don't have to do anything.

MACHOGOD: You can't do this to me. I'm disappointed in you. *(losing control)* I know what you've been doing. You've been fooling around, haven't you? You've been jumping into bed every chance you get.

SCOTT: Sure. Why not?

MACHOGOD: You're a slut. That's what you are. A common little slut.

SCOTT: Thanks.

MACHOGOD: *(catching hold of himself)* What am I saying? I'm sorry. You can't be a slut. You're a boy. (SCOTT *crosses to* SAL.

The MACHOGOD *crosses to* SEXGODDESS, *fuming)* How could you do this to the kid?

SEXGODDESS: Why not?

MACHOGOD: It's unnatural, that's what it is.

SEXGODDESS: He had it coming.

MACHOGOD: But this is overkill!

SEXGODDESS: Shh. This is the part where he has to tell his girlfriend.

SCOTT *mimes knocking on a door.* SAL *answers.*

SCOTT: Hello.

SAL: *(unenthused)* Oh, hi.

SCOTT: Uh, I think we need to talk.

SAL: What about?

SCOTT: You want to go for a drive?

SAL: Not particularly.

SCOTT: Well, could I come in?

SAL: Nope. Say what you want to say.

SCOTT: This is kind of awkward....

Pause.

SAL: What? (!)

SCOTT: Uh... I'm going to tell you something that will be totally difficult for you to believe.

SAL: I don't have time for this. I've got a history test tomorrow.

SCOTT: Wait. *(deep breath)* I'm pregnant.

SAL: Come on, Scott. What's going on? I've got to study.

SCOTT: I'm telling you the truth.

SAL: Oh, I get it. *(calling past him)* You can come out now. Game over. Big laugh. Haw haw. *(nobody responds)* So where are your buddies?

SCOTT: What buddies?

SAL: There's a bunch of your gang hiding back there, right? What was it? Look at the easy score? It wasn't enough you had to tell everybody what we did –

SCOTT: I didn't tell anybody….

SAL: Don't lie. Things always get back.

SCOTT: I'm sorry.

SAL: What kind of stupid joke is this? What if I'd really gotten pregnant?

SCOTT: Somebody really did.

SAL: Scott, you've gone off the deep end.

SCOTT: No I haven't. It's some amazing thing of medical science. I've seen the doctor.

SAL: So why come to me? No, this is impossible.

SCOTT: No, look – I've read up on it. It's not altogether impossible. A fertilized ovum – that's the little egg…

SAL: I know what an ovum is.

SCOTT: Yeah, well anyway it can be attached to any internal organ – (*He pats his stomach*) male or female – and it'll form its own whatever. (SAL *backs away from him*) It's been done, in laboratories, with animals.

SAL: That makes you a logical choice. (*He gives up and waits*) Okay, if I play along for the sake of an argument – what? So what?

SCOTT: So the ovum in this case had to be yours. I don't know how it got in here, but it's yours.

SAL: Who says?

SCOTT: I do.

SAL: How do I know who you've been sleeping with?

SCOTT: I haven't been…

SAL: How do I know?

118

SCOTT: Come on. That's not fair.

SAL: You did it with me, right? You could do it with anybody.

SCOTT: Not in this case.

SAL: That's what they all say.

SCOTT: Don't you trust me?

SAL: Scott... buzz off. (*She turns and mimes slamming the door in his face*)

SEXGODDESS: Hah hah!

SCOTT: Wake me up. I don't like this dream.

MACHOGOD: What are you laughing about?

SEXGODDESS: I've wanted to do this for a long time.

MACHOGOD: I'm glad somebody's happy. What's next?

SEXGODDESS: I guess he tells his parents.

The GODS *become father and mother.* SCOTT *has just told them.*

MACHOGOD: You are what?

SEXGODDESS: How could you do this to us?

MACHOGOD: How could you do it to yourself!

SEXGODDESS: How – *embarrassing.* I am absolutely mortified.

MACHOGOD: Didn't you take any precautions?

SEXGODDESS: Why did you do it at all! Don't you have any sense of morality? What am I going to tell your grandmother?

MACHOGOD: You'll have to leave town. If word gets out about this you'll be the laughing stock of the city.

SEXGODDESS: We'll be the laughing stock of the – oooh!

MACHOGOD: Well, you asked for it, you little fool.

SEXGODDESS: Wearing those tight Levis all the time...

SCOTT: Hey, wait a minute! (*parents are silent*) Aren't you forgetting something?

SEXGODDESS: Oh my gosh! The baby!

MACHOGOD: You're not going to keep it.

SEXGODDESS: I'm too young to be a grandmother!

MACHOGOD: Why not give it to some wonderful couple out there who are just begging to adopt –

SEXGODDESS: Why not put it in a foster home until you're old enough to –

MACHOGOD: Why not get married?

SEXGODDESS: Why not get an abortion?

SCOTT: Why not back off? Please, give me some room. Don't you think I've thought about this already? I've been going around this over and over again.

BOTH GODS: Well?

SCOTT: I can't make up my mind. (*the parents are about to explode*) Wait. (*pause*) Alright. Listen. I have to go through with it. (*a flash of the old* SCOTT) I mean, why should I deprive the world of a kid who might turn out like me? Hey!

MACHOGOD: Heaven help us.

SEXGODDESS: (*misty eyed*) Oh, Scott.

SCOTT: But you'll help, won't you? You've gotta help.

SEXGODDESS: Of course, dear – just let us get over our shock and we'll be right in there with you, won't we, Henry? (*pause*) Henry.

MACHOGOD: Whatever you say, Honeybun.

SCOTT: Thanks you guys. It'll be okay. (*pause*) I hope.

SEXGODDESS: Sure it will.

They reconcile and then the GODS *revert to themselves.*

SCOTT: Pretty soon I was experiencing everything that pregnant women experience. Every day I was sick to my stomach – I'm not sure why. I think it was the idea of having a baby. My legs started to ache. I couldn't eat a hot dog without getting heartburn. Then almost overnight, that part all cleared up and I felt like doing things.

SEXGODDESS: (*as store clerk*) Yes, may I help you? Oh, it's you, young man.

SCOTT: Yep.

SEXGODDESS: This is infantwear. You probably want the sports department.

SCOTT: No, this is (*sigh*) where I want to be.

SEXGODDESS: Is there anything I can show you?

SCOTT: Yeah. Something cheaper.

SEXGODDESS: (*archly*) We don't have anything cheaper. Quality baby clothes are expensive.

SCOTT: But this is just a little – a little –

SEXGODDESS: Fuzzy wuzzy pajamas. Aren't they cute?

SCOTT: And these things…

SEXGODDESS: Booties?

SCOTT: I wouldn't pay this much for my own shoes –

SEXGODDESS: I suppose not.

SCOTT: And how long does it take to grow out of them?

SEXGODDESS: At least three weeks.

SCOTT: I can't believe this.

SEXGODDESS: You can always go to Billy's Bargain Basement.

SCOTT: I've been to Billy's Bargain Basement.

SEXGODDESS: Perhaps you could afford a baby rattle –

SCOTT: (*suddenly still and wide eyed*) Oh gosh.

SEXGODDESS: What's the trouble?

SCOTT: Oh gosh.

SEXGODDESS: Young man?

SCOTT: It moved.

SEXGODDESS: I beg your pardon?

SCOTT: (*awestruck*) It's alive.

SEXGODDESS: What's alive?

SCOTT: Oh, uh – staying alive. "Staying alive, staying alive." It's an old song. (*trying another one*) "Alive alive oh."

SEXGODDESS: Do you have a pet hidden in your shirt?

SCOTT: No!

SEXGODDESS: We don't allow animals in the store.

SCOTT: Never mind, I was just leaving. (*He moves away from the saleswoman*) That is strange. And the strangest thing is that I'm finding it kind of – okay, laugh at me – but it's kinda great. I mean having a person growing inside of you. Except that I'm a boy. (*pause*) Of course my social life remains unaffected by all this.

SCOTT: Hey, Steriko – how are you?

MACHOGOD: (*as friend*) Hey Scott. Where y'been hiding?

SCOTT: Uh…

MACHOGOD: Look, are you free tonight?

SCOTT: What's up?

MACHOGOD: Bulletbrain has a new dirt bike. Everybody's going out to the quarry for a test run, so to speak.

SCOTT: Sounds great! Uh, maybe I'd better forget it.

MACHOGOD: Tomorrow's a party at my place – basherama – my parents are out of town. Guaranteed puke out.

SCOTT: Another time, okay?

MACHOGOD: What? I can't believe my ears. Scott Staples turning down a chugalug?

SCOTT: How are the guys?

MACHOGOD: Horny as usual. Hey, Saturday night… listen – cruise night on the main drag. See what's on display – maybe pick up a little fresh female whatever.

SCOTT: Oh.

MACHOGOD: You're not interested.

SCOTT: I guess not.

MACHOGOD: I guess not. Alright. Don't call us, we'll call you. Gotten too big for us, right?

SCOTT: It's not like that!

MACHOGOD: Sure. Hey, actually you are looking a little chubby. Are you putting on weight, Scotty pie?

Leaves.

SCOTT: *(calling after him)* I'm just drinking too much beer. *(He addresses the audience)* – And sometimes I thought I was drunk or something. This couldn't really be happening. I kept wishing it would go away. But it didn't and it took too long to be a nightmare. It took nine months and then it happened. *(pause)* For the last couple of months I kept dragging myself around like I was carrying a truck. I wore big Hawaiian shirts and told everybody I was going in for Sumo wrestling. Then one morning I woke up and I felt like I was on energy overload. I had to do something – but what? What I did was very uncharacteristic. I cleaned up my room. My mother came in – watched me for a while and then called the doctor. Women know these things. I won't describe the gruesome details – except to say that it hurt – a lot and a long time. I had contractions – I sweated – I ranted. It was like some awful spasm of fate wanted to put me through everything a woman goes through. Never mind that it was biologically impossible. When I woke up after the operation they showed me Melissa. She was beautiful. *(the* GODDESS *mimes bringing a little bundle to* SCOTT*)* She was beautiful.

MACHOGOD: *(as father)* You know what you're letting yourself in for?

Tug of war with the baby.

SCOTT: I don't care.

MACHOGOD: You don't want to be a single teenage parent. You're throwing your life away. Give the child up.

SEXGODDESS: (*as mother*) No, no. I think we can handle it. (*snatching the baby*) Now just let me take care of her. Don't worry about a thing.

She puts it in a crib. The baby starts to cry.

SCOTT: Mom –

SEXGODDESS: Don't you bother. I'll take care of her. Oh you – has snookums gone wee-wee? Has snookums gone wee-wee? Well, us'll change snookums won't us – atta wittle girly – gaga googoo.

SCOTT: Mom –

SEXGODDESS: I raised you, didn't I? You turned out alright.

MACHOGOD: That's a laugh.

SCOTT: Mom –

SEXGODDESS: Wittle Mewissa wants a wittle bottwe – a wittle milky wilky? Alwight, Mewissa...

SCOTT *takes the baby and the bottle.*

SCOTT: (*to the baby*) Melissa.

SEXGODDESS: Don't hold her like that.

SCOTT: My little girl. I'll do what's right for you, honest.

SEXGODDESS: Give me the bottle. Don't feed her like that. Give her to me. Honestly!

SCOTT: I can handle her – she's –

SEXGODDESS: Horsefeathers, you can handle her. What do you know about babies?

SCOTT: I can learn.

MACHOGOD: Let your mother do it. You're just a kid – and you're a boy. If you knew anything you wouldn't be in this mess. I oughta lay you over my knee.

SEXGODDESS: Oh, leave him alone. He was just trying to help.

MACHOGOD: Shut up. If you're so smart why didn't you raise him better?

SEXGODDESS: You shut up! He'll turn out alright!

MACHOGOD: When?

SCOTT: I'll take care of her.

SEXGODDESS: What?

SCOTT: You heard me. I'll take care of her in my own way.

SEXGODDESS: You can't even keep your room clean!

SCOTT: I'm moving out.

MACHOGOD: Oh great – and leave us with the brat.

SCOTT: Are you crazy? I wouldn't leave her here –

SEXGODDESS: Oh, my little boy – how will you live?

MACHOGOD: You move out and you won't get a cent from me.

SCOTT: Welfare.

MACHOGOD: Alright, there's the door.

SEXGODDESS: Henry! How could you – my two little babies…

MACHOGOD: They'll be back, don't worry. Nothing like a dose of cold reality to cure that kind of nonsense.

They revert to their divine selves.

MACHOGOD: This isn't fun anymore.

SEXGODDESS: It never really was.

The baby is crying. SCOTT *is trying to study.*

SCOTT: Melissa, what's wrong, honey. You're not wet. You're not hungry. So what's wrong? (*growing hysterical*) Calm down. Calm down. Don't you understand? Daddy's got a final tomorrow. I don't know the stuff. Quiet, alright? Quiet. I can't keep my head straight with you screaming like that. Shut up, you dumb kid! (*He has shocked even himself*) I'm sorry. I'm sorry, Melissa. I didn't mean that. It's not your fault. Hey, look what I got for you today. (*He takes out a real baby's rattle. The baby stops crying and starts to make happy noises*) That's better. (*pause*) I just get so tired, Melissa. And things seem so awful right now. You've got that awful baby sitter, the only one I can afford. And I have to study. I can't play with you all the time 'cause if I don't study I won't get a job and if I don't get a job things might not get any better and I might not be able to keep you and for sure I won't be able to give you all the things you need for the next whole lot of years. (*pause*) Hey, come on. I'm going to do it for you, kid. You're going to be a wonderful human being. Wonderful, yes you are! (*pause*) What's wonderful? You don't know what wonderful is? Let's see. How about happy – bright – strong – no pushover – just your own self, okay? That's what wonderful is, Melissa – that's what it is.

The GODS *move into the scene.*

SEXGODDESS: I'm amazed. The kid has something going for him after all.

MACHOGOD: Well, the girl certainly got the last laugh. I'll put a giant billboard up on Olympus announcing that you were the winner.

SEXGODDESS: How have I won?

MACHOGOD: You've turned him into a snivelling, unhappy, oppressed single teen parent. I never thought it would happen. The guy has turned responsible.

SEXGODDESS: Anything wrong with that?

MACHOGOD: Boys should have a good time.

SEXGODDESS: What about girls?

MACHOGOD: Them too – alright. So you've won.

SCOTT: I love you, Melissa. But I sure wish I could have been ready for all of this.

SEXGODDESS: Alright. Crank it back.

MACHOGOD: Time only goes one way. You can't rewind it.

SEXGODDESS: Wanta bet?

MACHOGOD: How much? (*thinks better*) No, never mind.

SEXGODDESS: Crank it back!

She snaps her fingers. SCOTT *spins around. The baby disappears.*
SALLY *enters.* SCOTT *sits beside her with his arm around her shoulders.*

SAL: Why are you putting all this pressure on me?

SCOTT: I'm not putting any pressure on you. I'm just trying to figure out why you're putting so much pressure on yourself.

SAL: I like you a lot, Scott. I told you. You don't turn me off. Not at all.

SCOTT: Then what are we waiting for? Hey, we've got a good thing going here. You don't want to break it up, do you?

SAL: No.

SCOTT: Then come on. Don't worry. I'll take care of you. It'll be great. Don't worry.

SAL: Scott...

SCOTT: Trust me.

The SEXGODDESS *tosses the baby rattle into the scene.*

SAL: What's that?

SCOTT: *(dazed)* Melissa?

SAL: Melissa? Who's she? Scott...

SCOTT: No, no – she's my little girl.

SAL: What?

SCOTT: I mean if I had a little girl I'd call her Melissa.

SAL: It's a nice name.

SCOTT: Strange. I must have blanked out for a second. What were we doing?

SAL: This.

Kiss.

SCOTT: Right. Just this.

SAL: Yeah. *(long kiss)*

END

Men and Angels

Lynn Kirk

MEN AND ANGELS WAS ORIGINALLY
written as an exercise for a drama class I was taking for my English
degree at the University of Regina. The assignment was, as I recall,
to "write a short stage play where the set serves as a metaphor for
the action." I thought of the way in which so many seemingly
"free" people lead caged lives, afraid to break out and take control
of their destinies. In this play the jail cell with its wide-open door
symbolizes that, although both characters are in prisons of their
own making, the key to a full and liberated life lies in their own
hands. A Saskatchewan Playwright Centre workshop helped to
shape this final draft of *Men and Angels*. The play won an Honorable
Mention in the 1987 Saskatchewan Drama Association Playwriting Competition.

Lynn Kirk lives in Regina where she writes short fiction and drama
for all media. Her radio play *Woman of Merit* won a CBC Literary
Competition award for comedy-drama and was produced on
"Morningside."

CHARACTERS

PENNY: An attractive, somewhat brassy woman in her mid-thirties. She wears tight, colourful clothes, perhaps high heels. She has a good-natured, matter-of-fact air.

JASE: A young man in his late twenties. He wears tailored slacks and an expensive sports shirt. He is an ordinary, nice-looking fellow, but needs a shave and looks ill. He has a bad hangover.

SET DESCRIPTION

Interior, police station/office in the fictitious village of Maisend. One portion of the stage is occupied by a barred cell in which bed, table, chair with jacket on it, toilet, sink or wash stand, and mirror are plainly revealed. The main room has a door leading outside, a desk with telephone, chairs, closet with cleaning supplies, and file cabinets. The walls hold a mirror, calendar, large map, posters, notices. In the cell Jase sleeps on the bed. It is important that the cell door, once opened, stays open, but that Jase doesn't leave the cell until his final dismissal. Penny undertakes cleanup duties such as sweeping, dusting, polishing, throughout much of the play.

Scene One

Penny enters wearing a shoulder-bag, carrying a tray with covered plate, coffee pot, mug, orange juice and cutlery. She slides her bag off, takes a key from a drawer, then walks to the cell. She sniffs the air and whistles to herself.

PENNY: Whew! What a snootful! *(she unlocks the cell door and props it open with a chair)* Okay mister. Wakey-wakey! Greet the dawn! *(JASE groans)* C'mon now. Get it while it's hot.

JASE: Go away!

PENNY: Nope. Hit the deck.

He struggles upright.

JASE: Oh, God. I'm dying.

PENNY: Sorry to tell ya... you're not. C'mon now. A little juice, little coffee, few scrambled eggs... *(sets the tray on the table)* C'mon. You'll feel better.

JASE: Y'got some Aspirin? Bromo maybe?

PENNY: I'll take a look. *(rummages in her purse, finds a small bottle)* Aspirin. You're in luck.

JASE: Oh, yeah. *(JASE struggles to the basin, splashes water on his face, looks in mirror over sink, examines tongue)* Oh, God.

PENNY: C'mon. Eat some breakfast.

JASE: Where am I?

PENNY: You're in jail.

JASE: Yeah, yeah. But where.

PENNY: Maisend.

JASE: *Mais*-end? You're kidding!

PENNY: Would I kid about a thing like that?

JASE: Oh, God. *(pause)* How'd I get here? Car?

PENNY: Beats me. I didn't *see* an extra car around.

JASE: It's ... Thursday, right?

PENNY: Nope. Saturday. (*consults calendar*) The twenty-first.

JASE: Twenty-first? (*pause*) Oh, God. (*pours Aspirins into his hand, tosses them down with his orange juice*)

PENNY: Saturday's how come I'm here. Herb... he's the cop... he coaches kids' baseball Saturdays.

JASE *begins to poke at the food.* PENNY *starts cleaning.*

JASE: He your husband?

PENNY: Haw! Naw, my brother. Baby brother.

JASE: You a policewoman or something?

PENNY: Something. I'm the cleaning lady. You make a break for it, I drop you with my broom.

JASE: Do you know... uh, Miss...

PENNY: Penny.

JASE: Okay, Penny. Do you know if... Herb, is it? If he got in touch with anyone for me?

PENNY: Must of. Said a lawyer's coming to bail you out.

JASE: Yeah. Okay.

PENNY: You don't sound surprised. (*pause*) This isn't a new scene with you, eh?

JASE: Look, lady, just sweep the floor.

PENNY: Okay!... damn touchy... try to be nice...

JASE: Look, I'm sorry, okay? It's the head, you know?

PENNY: Yeah, I know. Feel any better?

JASE: Some. Good coffee.

PENNY: I have a knack.

JASE: Good eggs too. Not too dry.

PENNY: I like to cook. It's sort of a business *and* a pleasure, you know?

JASE: You do all the cooking for the... uh, visitors here?

PENNY: Hardly a full-time job. You're the first one since... hmm ... April, I guess.

JASE: Ah. April. " ... the cruellest month... "

PENNY: April? No, April's usually pretty good around here. Meadowlarks, a nice rain... Now, you take *February* – that's cruel!

JASE: I wasn't talking about the weather. It's more... how it makes you feel inside. "April is the cruellest month, mixing memory with desire... "

PENNY: That poetry?

JASE: Ooh, yes. Yes, indeedy.

PENNY: Doesn't rhyme. *(pause) You* didn't write it, did you?

JASE: Huh! Afraid not.

PENNY: Sounds like you wish you did.

JASE: Yeah, well... if wishes were horses....

PENNY: Then beggars would ride! My ma used to say that. *(pause, remembering)* I used to think about it when I was a kid, day-dreaming, you know. Dozens of pretty horses racing around the track, with wishes hanging on them... instead of numbers. Coloured signs that said "money," or "happiness," or "beauty," *(pause)* "Love." Just grab a wish and jump on!

JASE: So which one would you grab?

PENNY: *(snaps back to present)* Good grief, who knows? Long time ago.

JASE: People don't stop wishing.

PENNY: Yeah, well, now I wish on stars. Star light, star bright. That's how you spend your nights in Maisend.

JASE: So then, nights in Maisend... what do you wish?

PENNY: I wish that Kevin Costner develops a big craving for small town jail cleaners. And just as he's pounding on my door I win the six-forty-nine... a big one, ten or twelve million.

JASE: Reasonable. Reasonable. Go on.

PENNY: And then for my third wish... Lord, listen to me! What do you care anyway? You don't know me from Adam's off ox.

JASE: I love to hear people's fantasies. They fascinate me. So the third wish?

PENNY: Oh, I dunno. (*wanders to the mirror, adjusts her hair absently*) Hmm. What do I wish? ... To be somewheres else, maybe. Doin' something different. New name, for sure.

JASE: People always want to change their names. What's wrong with "Penny?"

PENNY: Sounds like a kid, doesn't it? People hear "Penny" they expect some cute little teenybopper. A cheerleader, maybe. Gimme a P, gimme an E!

JASE: Is it a nickname?

PENNY: Yeah. But the real one's worse.

JASE: What?

PENNY: Ugh. Penelope. (*she says it like "antelope"*) Can you believe it? I hate that damned name!

JASE: (*says it her way*) Penelope. Sounds like an over-ripe melon.

PENNY: I know. My mother saw it in a book. Just my luck... Penelope!

JASE: There was a famous lady once, spelled it the same but said it different. (*pronounces it in the classical manner*) Penelope. She was a queen.

Henceforth in the play, "Penelope" is pronounced classically.

PENNY: Penelope? Hoity-toity! (*savours it*) Penelope. That's kinda nice.

JASE: She was a good woman. "Immortals will fashion among earthly men a gracious song in honour of faithful Penelope."

PENNY: Whoosh! That's so nice. (*pause*) You a preacher, maybe?

JASE: God, no. I just remember that. Homer said it.

PENNY: Homer? Well… it's nice anyway. Faithful Penelope. (*suddenly embarrassed*) So. What do they call *you* when you're at home?

JASE: Jase. That's a nickname too. My name's Jason Cavalier.

PENNY: Hey! Just like the beer! (*she sings the jingle*) "You gotta have a Cava, a Golden Cavalier!"

JASE: (*sighs*) That's me.

PENNY: What d'ya mean, that's you?

JASE: What I mean is… that's my company. Cavalier Beer.

PENNY: Naw. C'mon. Serious. You're not kiddin' me?

JASE: Nope.

PENNY: You mean you *own* that company?

JASE: More or less.

PENNY: I'll be damned. Welcome to the Jails of the Rich and Famous! (*pause*) You sure don't *look* like a big wheel. You should have a three-piece suit, and a paunch, and a… pocket watch or somethin'.

JASE: You don't look like the cleaning lady. You should have stringy grey hair and… varicose veins.

They both laugh, which causes him to groan and hold his head again.

PENNY: You know, I don't get it. You should be in your penthouse right now, waiting for the butler to bring you a hair of the dog.

JASE: Hate to disappoint you. No penthouse, no butler. (*pause*) But speaking of, uh, hair of the dog, I don't suppose…

PENNY: Get real.

JASE: It couldn't hurt to ask.

PENNY: So. Mr. Executive. You get like this often?

JASE: Just what the hell is *that* supposed to mean?

PENNY: Ah, look. I'm sorry. Herb says I'm nosier than Pinocchio.

JASE *snorts.*

PENNY: Well. Do you?

JASE: Herb's right. Frankly, it's none of your business. *(pause)*
But no. I wouldn't say … often.

PENNY: But jeez. You wake up who knows where, in jail even …

JASE: … and someone makes a phone call, and our people take
care of things, and that's that.

PENNY: Really? That's that.

JASE: I feel like hell for a couple of days. That's it.

PENNY: It's a funny way to run a business.

JASE: Penelope my faithful, I don't *have* to run the business. At
least not yet. Uncle Percy, *he* of the pocket watch, has run it
just fine for fifteen fruitful years.

PENNY: Well, first you say it's *your* company, then it's your
uncle … what do *I* know?

JASE: Good ole Percy's been chairman of the board since my
father died. He holds my shares in trust 'til I'm thirty.
There's the problem. In one more year I'm supposed to get
fitted for that suit, wind up the watch, and get my act
together.

PENNY: And you don't want to.

JASE: And I don't want to. *(pause)* I'm really not cut out for it.

PENNY: Oh. What *are* you cut out for?

JASE: What I'm doing now.

PENNY: *(looks around at his surroundings)*   Wonderful.

JASE: C'mon. I don't mean getting swacked. *(pause)* I'm a writer.

PENNY: Hey, really? You mean like books and stuff? Stories?

JASE: Yeah, stories … poetry mostly though.

PENNY: I *knew* there was somethin' about you. Jeez, a writer!
(pause) You make a living off that?

JASE: Not yet … a person has to get established. It takes a while to get your foot in the door.

PENNY: I guess you don't have to worry anyway.

JASE: That's not the point. I'm just starting to hit my stride. I've got some great stuff in here! (*taps his forehead, groans again*) But I need time... quality time... to myself. How can I develop anything when I have to peddle beer all day?

PENNY: So don't do it.

JASE: Do what?

PENNY: Don't peddle the beer. No one's gonna hold a gun to your head!

JASE: I don't think you've been listening. I *have* to do it. It's there in black and white, right in the old man's will. When I'm thirty, I take over. Period.

PENNY: Sounds like a funny will to me.

JASE: Yeah, well, he was a funny man. About as funny as a baby's crutch!

PENNY: Sounds like *my* old man. He beat you up?

JASE: No, no. That would require some... involvement. (*pause*) He was an efficient man, my father. A self-*made* man, as he was so very fond of saying. Unlike lesser beings, he was always in perfect control. The venting of anger would be counter-productive.

PENNY: But he treated you bad.

JASE: He didn't treat me at all. (*pause*) I was his only son, Penny ... named for him and for *his* father. Jason Cavalier. The third. Once when I was around nine, and inconveniently home for Christmas, he introduced me to a guest as... "My son Justin... uh, Jason."

PENNY: Jesus.

JASE: I tried so hard, so hard. The bastard didn't even know my name! (*pause*) So... as you can see, we didn't have a *warm* relationship.

PENNY: Was he cold to everyone? Your mother?

JASE: Mother. Ah, yes. Well, Mother found vodka to be an effective antifreeze. (*archly*) "A quart a day keeps the shivers away."

PENNY: Is she still... ?

JASE: Living? Depends on your point of view.

PENNY: So she doesn't help with the business or anything?

JASE: Lord, no. Just good old Uncle Percy until... it's me. Hell!

PENNY *notices a snagged fingernail, gets a file from her purse, and sits at the cell door to repair nail.* JASE *paces.*

PENNY: So what are you supposed to do till you're thirty?

JASE: Prove myself. He said I'm supposed to prove myself!

PENNY: Why are you so upset?

JASE: Because I don't know what the hell it means! *This is me.* Why was that never good enough? *I* know who I am, what I am! I don't have to prove it!

PENNY: Calm down. Don't take it out on me.

JASE: Sorry. It's the head, you know?

PENNY: I know. Well, what d'ya have against the beer business anyway? A beer's saved *my* life more than once.

JASE: No, it's not that. It's just... stuck behind that desk all day, facts and figures, lunch at the club, dinners with the same predictable couples...

PENNY: Oh. You married?

JASE: (*leans on the bars again, looks through*) Not now. I'm free as a bird. Free as the wind.

PENNY: So I see.

JASE: (*realizes his position, drops his hands*) Yeah.

PENNY: You leave her, she leave you... ? Jeez, here I go again. I guess it's just... I'm interested in people, is all.

JASE: Let's say she developed other interests.

PENNY: Ah. She was runnin' around.

JASE: Well... not at first.

PENNY: You?

JASE: A person needs... something. *You* try living day in, day out, with someone who hates your guts!

PENNY: Aw, c'mon. People say "hate" pretty easy.

JASE: Hmm. Maybe hate's *not* it. Disgust? Betrayal? Whatever, a colossal disappointment *oozed* from each of her lovely pores.

PENNY: Maybe she expected too much, eh? My ma used to say, "Expect nothing. Then you'll never be disappointed."

JASE: Yes. Great expectations had Cecily. *And*, a wondrous knack for ignoring the nasty details. She knew the setup from the first – the will and all... her people talked to my people at length before this "merger" was finalized. But she expected more and more. All the "establishment" things... the black tie receptions, those eight-course dinners with Bitsy and Winny and... dear, dear Muffey!

PENNY: Muffey! Hah! But Cecily... that's a classy name.

JASE: I guess so. She's a classy lady. Aye, there's the rub.

PENNY: But there must of been some good times. You must of started out okay.

JASE: Yeah. The first couple of years *were* good... fun, really. I got to show her off, and there was a lot to show. We travelled mostly, hit the sun spots... Spain, Hawaii, Venezuela... you know.

PENNY: Oh, you bet.

JASE: It wasn't just frivolous. I was writing. Well, I was gathering material. Storing it away. (*He taps his head again*) I thought we had a good life. Nice apartment in Toronto, fun friends, condo on Maui...

PENNY: Jeez, what was her problem? Sounds like heaven to me. White beaches, music, sidewalk cafés....

JASE: To quote the lady, she wanted a "civilized existence." She had expected to be Mrs. Jason Cavalier the Third, and by God she was going to be. Or else.

PENNY: But she was.

JASE: No-no-no. Still just Jase Cavalier. Missing was the big estate on the lake, for instance... seats on the board of the museum, and the opera, and the National Gallery. She wanted position and power, and that takes the big bucks. So when someone made her a better offer, she took it.

PENNY: You didn't want any of those things?

JASE: Didn't want 'em, couldn't *have* 'em. Not yet. You can only buy so much on your expectations. The great bloody mausoleum she coveted for our "home" priced out at two-eight!

PENNY: Two... eight?

JASE: Two million eight hundred thousand dollars.

PENNY: Million? Two *million*? Dollars? Are you saying a house is worth... (*pause*) But what do *I* know? Maybe you could *afford*...

JASE: Hardly. I'm living on an allowance... like a kid, for God's sake. An *allowance* till I'm thirty!

PENNY: (*steps into the cell, lifts the jacket and examines its obvious quality*) Last allowance I got was fifty cents a week. How does yours stack up?

JASE: Why am I telling you any of this? You obviously don't give a sweet tweet!

PENNY: I'm just saying that my allowance got me to the Roxy for Saturday matinees. Didn't quite fly me to Spain.

JASE: Okay, okay, it's generous. Handsome, even.

PENNY: No kidding.

JASE: But not enough. Never enough for Cecily Wainwright Cavalier! The money's there, Penny, it's *coming*. Soon. (*pause*) And I was there. But she said she was wasting her best years. *Wasting*. She wouldn't wait.

PENNY: So good riddance. Good riddance to bad rubbish, that's what my ma would say.

JASE: Your "ma" was a bloody oracle, wasn't she! (*sees that* PENNY *is deeply wounded – pause*) Oh, hell. Sorry Penny. I'm just....

PENNY: Oh, I know. It's the head, right? Must be handy to have a week-long binge to hang your bad manners on. Big city gentleman!

JASE: It was a rotten thing to say. I know you meant well. Please forgive me.

PENNY: You shouldn't badmouth people you don't even know. When it came to mothers, I guess she could hold her own against... (*pointedly*) some others I could name!

JASE: I'm sure she was a fine woman.

PENNY: Fine? I don't know about fine. She worked hard. She did her best, I think, but...

JASE: Go on.

PENNY: Oh, I don't know. (*pause*) She was such a mixture. Funny.

JASE: Funny how?

PENNY: Well, strong and weak, I guess you could say. (*pause*) I remember one time the new teacher... it was a one-room school, you know... the new teacher thought my brother George had lice, 'cause he was scratching his head all the time. (*pause*) We were poor, all right, and it showed, but ma kept us clean... quite a trick in that shack with no runnin' water. (*pause*) Anyway, poor Georgie had eczema... had it from a baby... and there was no cortisone cream or like that in those days, believe me. So it got runny and itchy, and he had it bad in his hair. Tried to tell that dumb teacher, but she's goin' "Ooh! Lice!" (*pause*) So she grabs Georgie, and gets the basin and the tin of coal oil, and in front of the whole class she bends him over and pours coal oil all over his head. "Best thing to kill lice," she says. (*pause*) Stuff hit those sores on his head... and he screamed... and he screamed… and he got away from her and just sort of jerked around the front of the room, running into the desks and the walls, holding his head and screaming… like an animal. (*pause*) The next morning, Ma went two miles to Aunt Selma's to borrow a decent hat and some gloves, and then she came to the school. She walked down the centre aisle right in the middle of geography lesson. She stood real tall, holding her pocket book into her waist with both hands… I hardly recognized her, she looked like a scared rabbit at home… (*pause*) And she said, "Miss Perdue, I believe? *I* am Mrs. Maddon." Then she reached out, real calm, and jerked the bottom of the roll-down map of the world… you know, with the pictures of chocolate bars on the edges? … and it snapped up like a window blind and slapped around at the top like a whip cracking. (*pause*) Then she said, "I understand you have been improving my boy's hygiene." *Hygiene*, she said. "And I am here to tell you, Miss Perdue, that if you so much as raise an eyebrow to one of my children again, it will be the worse for you!" By God, I was proud of her that day!

JASE: So that's not a fine woman?

PENNY: Yeah, I guess. She did what she could for us kids. But… she could never stand up to Pa. Sometimes I hated her so bad for that. 'Course, I know better now, being a woman myself, but still…

JASE: Your father hard on her, eh?

PENNY: You know, in all his life I never heard him say one – not one – decent word to her. Did most of his talkin' with his fists.

JASE: He actually hit her?

PENNY: All the time. He knocked *us* around too, but mostly Ma. And she just took it, time after time. The worst time… (*pause*) Never mind.

JASE: What? Tell me.

PENNY: You'd laugh. It sounds funny now.

JASE: No, I won't. Go on.

PENNY: (*hesitates and then decides to take the plunge*) He hit her with a frozen fish.

JASE *snorts.*

PENNY: See?

JASE: You took me by surprise. A fish?

PENNY: Yeah. He'd been ice fishing with a couple of buddies, gone two or three days. He came home in the middle of the night, mean drunk – no surprise. Got Ma up to make some food, but she wasn't moving fast enough or something, so he slammed her one with a seven-pound pickerel.

JASE: Dear God.

PENNY: Yeah. Like a big cold rock with a handle. He clubbed her with it over and over… broke her jaw and her nose and her cheekbone. Never did heal right, neither.

JASE: I hope she pressed charges.

PENNY: Get serious. If she sent him up, he'd break more than her face when he came back!

JASE: She could have left.

PENNY: Left for where? With what? Take her five kids and her cardboard suitcase and check into the Ritz? *Real* life is mean, mister! Guess you didn't learn everything in your world travels!

JASE: I seem to be learning the hard way.

PENNY: (*softening*) Yeah, I guess… your wife and all.

JASE: Well. Water under the bridge. (*pause*) You married?

PENNY: Yes and no.

JASE: You must know yes or no.

PENNY: I knew sixteen years ago, but I couldn't tell you now.

JASE: He take a walk?

PENNY: Yep. Wandering Wayne. Just strolled out one night and didn't come back. Left me with a three-year-old kid, a pregnant dog, and two months rent due on the trailer. And that is the story of my life.

JASE: But sixteen years? A lot goes on in sixteen years. What's happened since then?

PENNY: Well... the trailer burned. All my stuff.... Wasn't up to much, I guess, but still... (*pause*) My boy Ken, he went to work on the oil rigs a while back.

JASE: I see. Two notable events in sixteen years.

PENNY: (*sardonically*) The dog died.

JASE: That's not what I mean and you know it. All that time... in *Maisend*?

PENNY: I keep busy.

JASE: Sure, cleaning an empty jail.

PENNY: No, I do lots of things. Herb there helped me set up in a big old house down the way, and when the drilling crews come through I give 'em room and board. That's good money!

JASE: But what about getting out, seeing people?

PENNY: I'm out lots. You heard of Mandy-Lou Jewelry? I'm top sales for this whole area. I do four, five jewellry parties a month. See these earrings? (*shows him*) This line's called "Golden Trap." Here's the pendant (*she lifts her necklace*) I model the stuff all the time 'cause it's good advertising... if I do say so myself.

JASE: But that's what I mean! For Pete's sake, you're an attractive woman! What about fun, or... or... romance?

PENNY: Huh! Romance he says!

JASE: C'mon Penny, you don't look like a nun to me. You must have dates and lots *of* them... a steady, maybe?

PENNY: (*wanders over to the mirror, looks in as she talks*) I've had my chances. Lots of chances. But... I don't want to get too serious. Once bitten, twice shy, my Ma... (*she stops, laughs self-consciously*)

JASE: I'm surprised you took the plunge in the first place, with your folks' example. Of course, *I* should talk.

PENNY: Guess I spent too many Saturdays at the Roxy. Things worked out lovely for Doris Day. Why not for me? *(pause)* Besides, I did my "Pillow Talk" a little early if you catch my drift. There were a couple of things that Doris forgot to tell me.

JASE: Trouble, eh?

PENNY: Yeah, that's what they called it. I shoulda known better. I *did* know better. But you know, that Wayne was the first person who ever treated me like I was worth somethin'. I woulda done anything for him.

JASE: But you didn't have to *marry* him!

PENNY: Huh-ho! Listen to him! What you mean is, *he* didn't have to marry me. *(pause)* But he did. And he did try. We both did. Our first couple of years were all right too. Wayne worked pretty steady at Jensen's garage. But then Jensen had a stroke and closed the place... and we were on the pogie, and things just started to fall apart. *(pause)* The responsibility got to him, I guess. We'd fight... and I'd cry and he'd cry and Kenny'd cry... Finally he just walked out... crying. He slammed the door and pounded the side of the trailer a couple of times, like to broke his hand. I heard him yell, "Shit!" *(pause)* And that's the last time I ever heard his voice.

JASE: You could've had him traced... for child support anyway.

PENNY: Hah! About two years later he sent a post card with big skyscrapers on the picture... from Detroit. He said *(she folds her hands in front of her and recites)* "This city is big. They make cars here. Hope you are fine I am too. Hey to Kenny and Blue." Blue was the dog. And that's it. *(pause) More* water under the bridge.

JASE: Yes, it is. So why don't you get on with it? Grab one of those oil drillers and start over! For Pete's sake, you could have a life! A full life!

PENNY: *(pause)* I just always thought... well... maybe he's gonna come back, you know?

JASE: *(pause)* Oh, Penny. He's not coming, Penny.

PENNY: I know.

There is an uncomfortable silence, then both rally visibly.

JASE: Look, you're not... how old are you, anyway?

PENNY: None of your... *(pause)*... thirty-six.

JASE: But see, that's young! You're in your prime! It's not too late, you can do anything you want! (PENNY *shrugs*) You know, people like you make me furious! Bloody doormats. You take all the crap life hands you, don't lift a finger to help yourself, and expect people to feel sorry for you!

PENNY: Wait a minute! I never said...

JASE: *(interrupting)* Rotting away in this burg is not some kind of *destiny*! Take charge! What's stopping you? Saint Augustine said it. Men are like the angels, he said. Men, and angels, have *free will*!

PENNY: There you go with that fancy talk again.

JASE: Penny, listen. It just means that you have a choice in your life.

PENNY: Speak for yourself. I'm not a man and I'm not an angel.

JASE: But do you want to spend the rest of your existence cleaning the jail? Seeing the same twenty-three people week in, week out?

PENNY: I guess not, but... I never really thought...

JASE: Time's a-wastin', kid!

PENNY: You're talking crazy.

JASE: What was that third wish? "Someplace else, doin' something different, new name for sure?"

PENNY: *(pause)* Penelope.

JASE: Exactly. Penelope... Maddon, moves to the city, where she makes and markets the world's best coffee. Or maybe she sells jewellery to the wives of visiting dignitaries. Or maybe she...

PENNY: *(interrupting)* You're nuts, y'know that?

JASE: Not me, baby. Grab one of those horses. Quick, here they come! Make your move... make a choice!

PENNY: I can't. I can't.

JASE: Give me strength. You are *not* your mother.

PENNY: But... *(pause)* That's right. That's right. Maybe... I've still got my looks.

JASE: You bet.

PENNY: I'm not afraid of hard work... *(pause)* Maybe I could!

JASE: That a girl!

PENNY: *(almost to herself)* There's my cousin Patsy, got a suite right downtown, maybe she'd put me up while I look for something. I could take the jewellry, do it on the side... *(pause, she turns to JASE)* What about you, Jase? Look what you could have goin' for ya! You're so smart, and you're *rich*! Talk about choices! Think what you've got stored up there. *(reaches in and taps his forehead)* You could be famous... you wouldn't have to prove anything ever again. That's freedom for ya!

JASE: *(going along with her)* It might work, Penny. It just might work. Because a person *can* choose! A person *must choose*! Penny, we play our cards right, *we could soar with the angels*!

The phone rings. At the sound, both go still. The excitement of the moment is lost.

PENNY: Hello? *(pause)* Trouble? No... everything's fine, why? *(pause)* Well, Herb, I can't help if I sound funny. What is it? *(pause)* Oh. You're kidding. Well. Okay then... *(pause)* No, I'll do it. G'bye. *(She replaces the phone, opens a drawer and pulls out a manila envelope, walks into the cell and puts the envelope on the table)* Here's your stuff. That was Herb. *(pause)* That lawyer fellow's here. Talked to Judge Crawford

... on a Saturday yet! You don't even have to appear. *(leaves the cell, swings the chair away from the cell door, and holds the door open for him)* So you're free to go. Sounds right, doesn't it? *Free* to go?

JASE: Yeah, sure.

In silence he puts on his jacket, opens the envelope onto the table, pockets his wallet and spare change. He leaves the cell, strapping on his watch as he passes Penny and heads for the outer door.

PENNY: Like you said... all the choices are there.

JASE: *(doesn't look at her)*   That's right. *(making a production of adjusting his watchband)*

PENNY: I'm gonna watch for your books.

JASE: *(stops with his back to her)*   Faithful Penelope. I wasn't quite truthful with you, you know.

PENNY: Oh Jase, please don't...

JASE: *(interrupting as he turns to look at her)*   St. Augustine and I parted company some time ago. I don't do this sometimes. I do this often. *Very* often.

PENNY: Please...

JASE: *You* spread those wings, honey. *Someone* has to soar.

JASE *exits.* PENNY *looks after him.*

PENNY: *(pause)*   Sure. If wishes were horses. *(walks into the cell, pushes the chair against the table, catches her reflection in the mirror, takes a critical look)* But you never know. *(leaves the cell, closing the barred door behind her. She leans against this door for a second. Then she retrieves her purse and heads for the outer door)* You just never know.

Exit.

END

No Means No!

Richard Frost, Greg Olson and Lyle Johnson

I CONCEIVED THIS PLAY IN THE winter of 1990-91 after discussion with some of my senior students. I wanted to do a play about something of interest and importance to young people with a goal of performing it in the Regional Drama Festival that year. Students and staff of the school were surveyed for their input and the cast contributed their ideas as the play evolved. Research was gained from guidance counsellors, the Moose Jaw Police Service, and the Saskatoon Rape Crisis Centre. We gratefully acknowledge their involvement.

Richard Frost and Greg Olson, two creative local people, were approached to put the ideas and facts into a script that would challenge the actors and audience with creative dialogue and an honest discussion of date rape. Many evaluations and rewrites later, the script has reached this point in its life. Congratulations guys!

A note to those staging the play: contemporary music and area lighting, as noted in the script, can enhance the production. Student input for music and current colloquialisms will give a contemporary feel to the piece and some ownership to the cast. Keep it current.

The rape scene is purposely done offstage to allow the audience to imagine what is happening. Nothing is as powerful as our personal view of this violent and brutal crime; putting it on stage would diminish the audience's contribution to the play – to say nothing of the staging difficulties that would be created. The sets should be minimal so that they may be changed quickly.

The time from conception to performance was a short two months. The dedication and commitment by the production team made this an exciting and challenging time. It prompted much discussion amongst those who viewed or performed it. North Battleford Comprehensive High School took it to regionals and provincials in 1992. Their input and suggestions for improvements have been considered in this published script. Thanks to their cast and teacher, Roy Challis.

Lastly, the play should be staged with honesty and sincerity. *No Means No!* discusses a situation we hope no one has to learn about first hand. The national average for reported rapes is estimated to be one in seven of those that occur. Openness and exposure can curtail this crime and, hopefully, stop it. If you know of an incident, help the person to understand it's not his/her fault and get them to professional help as quickly as possible. Counsellors, police, church, parents, and friends all can be of assistance – no one is alone. No really does mean No.

—Lyle Johnson, Drama Director, A.E. Peacock Collegiate

"No Means No" is the first play that Greg Olson has written. Olson grew up in Moose Jaw, Saskatchewan, and together with his wife and children, continues to call Moose Jaw home. Through his high school years at Central Collegiate, Greg was heavily involved in drama. Olson is currently the programming manager for Cable Television in Moose Jaw.

Richard Frost was born and raised in Swift Current, Saskatchewan, and now lives in Moose Jaw with his wife Nadia, and their dog, Shadow. He has been actively involved in all aspects of dramatic production since high school and continues to take part in theatrical practices through his work in community access programming with the local cable TV company and his volunteer time with Moose Jaw's community theatre group, Chocolate Moose.

PREMIERE PRODUCTION

The play was first performed March 27, 1991 by A.E. Peacock Collegiate as part of the Saskatchewan Drama Association Region 11 One-Act Festival. The following were members of the original production:

MELISSA . . . . Jodie Hendry
JENNIE . . . . Lianne Sagal
MUSIC TEACHER . . . . Herke Van Hulst
RICK . . . . Ian O'Brien
DAVE . . . . Stewart Skinner
D.J. . . . . John Evans
JANET (GIRL #1) . . . . Samira Azzahir
CANDI (GIRL #2) . . . . Krista Konkin
PATTY (GIRL #3) . . . . Patty Keach
ROCHELLE (GIRL #4) . . . . Rochelle Wendt
DAWN (GIRL #5) . . . . Medorann Harris
LAUREL (GIRL #6) . . . . Laurel Downey
KAYLA (GIRL #7) . . . . Robin Meuller
LEAH (GIRL #8) . . . . Leah Tressal
RACQUEL (GIRL #9) . . . . Jennie Grado
BRENDA-ANNE (GIRL #10) . . . . . . Laura Francis
CHAD (BOY #1) . . . . Chad Waughtal
MIKE (BOY #2) . . . . Mike Kreuger
CURTIS (BOY #3) . . . . Curtis Cole
JAKE (BOY #4) . . . . Evan Davis
MATT . . . . Matt Cowan
GREG . . . . Greg Kreuger
BRAD . . . . Ronley Arnold
DEANNA. . . . . Jody Ross
LORI . . . . Kendra Bliss

CHOIR MEMBERS, DANCE AND STUDENTS OF CASTLE ROCK HIGH: Joelle McBain, Stacy Johnson, Tanya Gammel, Sian Hanslow, Shari-Anne Charles, Carolyn Daly, Maria Mckenzie, Christine Martin, Adrienne Moffat, Shirl-lea Ann Gorgichuk, Crystal C. R. Bate, Angel Schroeder, Lanita Linsley, Cynthia Box, and Brenda Ward

THE CREW: David Smale, Kristi Vance, Mike Knelsen, Angela

Wendt, Nadine Koch, Jason Guenther, Gina Cornish, Georgette Stephens, Debbie Statham, Crystal McKenzie, Tasha Boorah, Trisha Booth, Colin Foster, and Corey La Buick

DIRECTOR .... Lyle Johnson
STAGE MANAGER .... Jenny MacFarlane
LIGHTING................. Kevin Coxe
SOUND .... Amanda Foster
SET .... Keith Littler
SCRIPT WRITERS .... Greg Olson, Richard Frost

Special thanks to these people who made the play possible: Lynn Park, Karen Francis, Michelle Free, Kelly Stokes, and the students and staff of A.E. Peacock Collegiate.

CHARACTERS

MELISSA: *A good, friendly grade 11 student*

JENNIE: *Melissa's best friend*

RICK: *Cool, attractive grade 11 student*

DAVID: *Nice, average grade 11 student*

MR./MS. NELSON: *Director of school choir*

DJ: *Aggressive disc jockey*

GIRLS #1 - 10

BOYS #1- 4

BRAD: *Linebacker on the football team*

DEANNA ROSS: *Intoxicated girl at the dance*

LORI: *Girl in daring outfit at the dance*

MATT: *Shy boy who lacks confidence*

GREG: *Matt's friend*

The cast may be expanded to include students in the hallways, at the dance, and in the choir.

Scene One

THE CHOIR REHEARSAL: *A music room. We hear the first verse of "Amazing Grace" as the lights come up on a choir of ten to twenty students.* DAVID, JENNIE, *and* MELISSA *are in the choir, with* MELISSA *in the centre of the group.*

CHOIR:

> Amazing grace! How sweet the sound,
> That saved a wretch like me!
> I once was lost, but now am found,
> Was blind, but now I see.

DIRECTOR: Sounds good people, sounds good. Melissa, your solo is coming along fine. I know we've been rehearsing every night, but it just needs a little more. We still need to focus on meaning and feeling, people. Think about what you are saying. Don't forget, our concert is in seven days. Your performance will reflect your rehearsing. Next rehearsal is Tuesday at 7:30 in the auditorium, be on time. Any questions?

VOICE IN CHOIR: Do we have to wear those choir robes from the last century?

DIRECTOR: No, we're raising money for something from this century. For now, wear something formal, no jeans, spandex, or sweats. Great. That's all. *(Choir begins to disperse)*

JENNIE: Good singing. Ever think of changing your name?

MELISSA: What would I change it to?

JENNIE: I don't know... Celine?

MELISSA: As in Dion?

JENNIE: Yeah! *(laughter)*

DAVID: Your solo was awesome, Melissa. You did great.

MELISSA: Thanks, David. See you later.

MELISSA *and* JENNIE *sit to chat for a bit.*

DAVID: You bet. Bye Jennie.

JENNIE: Bye David. (*after he leaves*) He is such a babe!

MELISSA: I knew it.

JENNIE: What?

MELISSA: You've got the hots for David.

JENNIE: Not the hots. I just think he's cute, that's all. (*pause*) Okay, okay, I admit it. David is one hot man.

MELISSA: Why don't you talk to him? Tell him how you feel.

JENNIE: Melissa, every girl knows that's not how it works. You can't be obvious or else guys won't go for you. You have to make them think you're not interested so they'll try even harder to make you notice them.

MELISSA: Stop living in the dark ages, Jen. Just tell him how you feel. Honesty works these days. Trust me.

JENNIE: Well, we'll see. Pick you up for the movie at the usual time?

MELISSA: No, not tonight. I've decided to go to the school dance.

JENNIE: You what? You've never been to a school dance in your life.

MELISSA: That's exactly why I'm going. I'm in grade 11, I want to go to a school dance for once. If I like it, I'll go more in my senior year. Everybody talks about what goes on there.

JENNIE: But it's the movie of the year and it's your turn to buy the jumbo popcorn.

MELISSA: There'll always be movies. I've been going to the same place with the same people at the same time forever now. I just want some variety in my Friday nights. Next week, I'll be back with greasy jumbo popcorn in one hand and a diet coke in the other, but tonight (MELISSA *strikes a tango pose*) I dance!

JENNIE: (*laughing*) I was wrong about you, Melissa.

MELISSA: How so?

JENNIE: Maybe you should change your name to Janet.

MELISSA and JENNIE: As in Jackson.

They laugh and exit.

SCENE TWO

THE DANCE: *High school gymnasium. Music up immediately, to cover change. Lights up when stage is set. Song ends. Total music is thirty to forty seconds. Typical dance with girls clustering together in groups and guys hanging out. There is lots of dancing.*

D.J.: Are you having a good time?

CROWD: Yeah! Woo! Woo! Woo! Woo!

D.J.: I can't hear you!

CROWD: *(repeats, louder)* Yeah! Woof! Woof! Woof!

D.J.: All right! Now it's time to "Wiggle It!" *(title of a popular song)*

Music up. DAVE *enters.* RICK *enters from opposite direction.* RICK *is clean cut, self-assured, running for student president. They meet at centre after greeting friends on the way.*

RICK: Hey man, what's up?

DAVE: Not much. Where did you disappear to for so long?

RICK: I just went out for some "air."

DAVE: Yeah sure, Rick. We can all smell that forty proof "air" on your breath. Did you save any for your friends?

RICK: I even brought a little "fresh air" with me. *(He laughs and produces a small flask)*

DAVE: Are you nuts! You want to get caught and kicked out of school?

RICK: Relax, lots of people get away with it.

They move downstage. RICK *takes a swig and eventually gets* DAVE *to take a small sip as a group of girls walks across stage.* MELISSA *is among them.*

RICK: Hey Melissa. Where are you going?

MELISSA: Just going to the washroom.

RICK: Don't be too long. Come talk to me when you get back.

The whole group of girls exits to the bathroom. We see a student stumble to her feet, then run in the same direction that the girls exited. The group of girls comes running back, squealing.

GIRL #1: Yuck! Is that ever gross!

GIRL #3: Deanna just puked on the principal.

GIRL #2: What an idiot!

Girls move from focus and gossip.

DAVE: Smooth move.

Slower song comes up and MELISSA *moves to* RICK.

MELISSA: This is one of my favourite songs. Come on Rick, let's dance.

She pulls him out onto the dance floor.

DAVE: You'd better watch her, Rick. She's after you! (*as* RICK *and* MELISSA *move away*) Did you see that look she gave him? She's got the hots for Rick.

MELISSA: You've been drinking, haven't you? You smell like a brewery.

RICK: I only had one drink before the dance. You're not an undercover cop or anything, are you?

MELISSA: Just dance with me before the song ends.

They dance. Focus changes to a group of girls near the bleachers.

GIRL #1: Looks like a certain couple is enjoying themselves.

GIRL #2: Who?

GIRL #3: Melissa and Rick.

GIRL #4:   Oh!

GIRL #1:   She's so lucky. He's so hot!

GIRL #3:   I wish I was in Melissa's shoes.

GIRL #2:   Why?

GIRL #3:   He's only the cutest grade 11 in the school. Where have you been?

GIRL #2:   Well, I've been…

BRAD *crosses, walking in an exaggerated "jock walk."*

GIRL #4:   She's got the hots for Brad.

GIRL #3:   The Neanderthal linebacker?

She imitates BRAD's *walk and the girls all laugh and "bug"* GIRL #2.

GIRL #4:   It's too bad he wouldn't give any of us the time of day.

GIRL #1:   Rick sat across from me in English class.

ALL GIRLS: Ooooh!

They fade back into the dance. A second group of girls emerges from the crowd.

GIRL #5:   I can't stand it anymore. Why won't Chris ask me to dance? I've sent him all kinds of signals.

GIRL #6:   He's such a jerk. Can't he see that you like him?

GIRL #7:   Yeah! It's sort of obvious.

GIRL #5:   Oh well, there's plenty of guys out there. I can live without dancing with Chris.

GIRL #8:   Here comes just one of those many guys!

They all laugh as a boy obviously lacking in confidence approaches.

GIRL #9:   Hold me back!

GIRL #10:   Come on now, I saw him first.

They laugh. The boy loses courage and turns back into the crowd.

GIRL #5:   Why doesn't Chris ask me to dance?

GIRL #10: Would you just go over and ask him?

GIRL #5: Are you kidding? I couldn't do that.

GIRL #10: Come on. We're going to talk to Chris.

She grabs GIRL #5 *and drags her off.*

GIRL #5: How can you...

GIRL #9: Did you see Lori? Who's she trying to impress with that dress?

GIRL #8: And those shoes do not go with that outfit.

GIRL #7: Nice try.

GIRL #9: Look, here she is!

A girl walks by wearing a daring outfit. The group is quiet until she has passed by.

GIRL #9: What a ho'!

GIRL #6: I can't believe she'd wear that to a dance.

GIRL #8: It's kind of obvious what she's after tonight.

GIRL #7: Hey, that's Melissa out there dancing with Rick.

GIRL #6: You're right! What's she doing here? She never comes to school dances.

GIRL #7: Yeah, I don't think I've ever seen her at one before.

GIRL #9: Looks like she's making up for lost time.

Focus of scene shifts to RICK *and* MELISSA *as they stop dancing.*

MELISSA: You look kind of pale. Are you feeling okay?

RICK: Not great. It's hot in here, isn't it?

MELISSA: Maybe we should get some fresh air.

RICK: Fresh air. Yeah. Fresh air's a good idea.

The girls huddle together to gossip about the two leaving. Lights down on the dance scene as the music starts to fade.

Scene Three

THE RAPE: *Bench – front lawn of the school.*

RICK: Let's sit here for a minute.

MELISSA sits. RICK sits beside her on the bench.

MELISSA: One drink, eh?

RICK: Yeah, just one.

He leans his head back, stretches out his arms in what's an obvious move to get his arm around MELISSA. BRAD and GIRL enter.

MELISSA: Well, that was smooth, Romeo.

RICK: I thought so.

BRAD and GIRL walk in front of bench.

BRAD: Rick, Melissa.

MELISSA and RICK: Hi.

BRAD and girl exit.

MELISSA: *(pause)* So have you had enough fresh air?

RICK: Not quite. Just sit here with me a little longer.

MELISSA: We should get back... *(RICK kisses her)*

RICK: *(pause)* Are you sure you want to go back in?

MELISSA: Well, maybe not just yet. *(They kiss again)*

RICK: So how come you never come to dances?

MELISSA: I don't know. I didn't think I'd have a good time, I suppose.

RICK: Are you having a good time?

MELISSA: Yeah, I am.

They kiss for the third time, a little longer than before, then break away. There is an uncomfortable pause.

RICK: It sure is a beautiful night.

MELISSA: Yeah. It's really nice.

RICK: (*pause*) Hey. The stars are great tonight. Have you ever just looked at the stars?

MELISSA: Lots of times. I like to lie in my backyard and try to find constellations. (*pointing*) There's the Big Dipper, that one's easy. The Little Dipper is harder.

RICK: You have to find the North Star, don't you?

MELISSA: Yeah, but how?

Pause. RICK *pulls* MELISSA *up.*

RICK: Come here. Over here.

MELISSA: Why?

RICK: It's darker. (*pulls her into darkness*) You can see the stars better when you're out of the light.

MELISSA: First it's fresh air, now it's stars. Are you turning into some kind of nature boy?

RICK: Come over here.

MELISSA: Rick, I... (*silence as he apparently kisses her*) I think we should go back now!

RICK: Why?

MELISSA: Well. To dance. That's what we came for, isn't it?

RICK: Is it?

Pause.

MELISSA: Rick, don't.

RICK: Why not? Come on Melissa.

MELISSA: Rick! I don't want to. I want to go in now. (*pause*) Get your hands away. Stop it!

DAVID *enters into the pool of light.*

MELISSA: Rick, please. I said stop it. I don't want...

DAVID *stops.*

RICK: Melissa! I know what we both want.

MELISSA: Get off me. Stop it! Please… Stop it! No, no, no…
   (starts to cry)

Those are the last words we hear from offstage. DAVID *is frozen. There is never-ending silence.* RICK *walks to bench and sits, tucking in his shirt as he turns around to see* DAVID *standing there.*

RICK: Hey, David. What are you doing?

DAVID: Nothing. I didn't see anything.

RICK: What are you talking about?

DAVID: Nothing.

RICK: *(to* DAVID*)* Let's get back to the dance. Somebody is sure to be wondering where we are. *(whispering)* Hey Melissa. See you inside. Okay?

DAVID *goes into the dance.* RICK *follows.* MELISSA *is heard sobbing softly. Lights dim slowly as sobbing fades.*

Scene Four

THE TELEPHONE CALL: MELISSA *and* JENNIE*'s bedrooms – split stage. Lights up.* MELISSA *is still sobbing. Scene opens with phone ringing several times.* MELISSA *is wearing a housecoat wrapped tightly. She hesitates before answering.*

JENNIE: Hello, Melissa?

MELISSA: Hello.

JENNIE: Where've you been? I've been trying to get hold of you for the last hour.

MELISSA: Well… I was in the shower.

JENNIE: For an hour? You must look like a prune. *(*MELISSA *is silent)* It was a joke… *(pause)* I'm dying to know…. How was the dance last night? Was it everything you thought it would be? *(silence)* Well, I'm waiting. Tell me everything.

MELISSA: I don't want to talk about it right now.

JENNIE: It went that well, eh? What happened? (*silence*) What happened? Were there lots of people? Should I go to the next one? Did he drive you home? I just love his car. Did he kiss you goodnight? (*pauses, expecting an answer*) Melissa. You were really excited about this dance. Talk to me. How was it?

MELISSA: The dance was okay. It just.... It wasn't what.... How was the movie?

JENNIE: You should have seen Brenda spill her popcorn on that guy from Riverside. (*or name of other rival high school*) The one she likes? Her face went as red as the seats and his shirt was covered in simulated butter stains. We almost got kicked out when the guy threatened to whip us with his red licorice. Don't bother seeing the movie though. It was really stupid. (*silence*) Anyway, Brenda phoned and she wants to go hang out at the mall this afternoon. She probably figures on seeing that Riverside guy at the drycleaners or something. You want to come along?

MELISSA: No. I don't feel like it today.

JENNIE: Are you okay? Melissa?

MELISSA: I've got to go.

MELISSA *hangs up phone.* JENNIE *hangs up and begins dialing again.* MELISSA *stands beside the phone for a moment, then picks up the clothes that she wore to the dance and crosses to another area where a garbage can is located. She strikes a match as the telephone starts to ring and the lights fade.*

SCENE FIVE

THE HUMILIATION: *The school, Monday morning.*

ANNOUNCEMENTS: Good morning. Today is day four. Congratulations to the new student council: Rick Gilmore, President; Sandy Smithers, Vice-president; Elizabeth Watkins, Secretary; Allen Martin, Treasurer; and Audrey

McArthur, Social Convenor. First meeting will be held today at 12:05 in room 107. Please be on time. Also, Dave Helland and Andrea Berger report to the counselling center before classes this morning. And finally, the following students please report to the office: Carla Lawrence, Eileen Casavant, Amanda Haner, Tara Clark, Darren Utley, and Todd Fitzpatrick. Thank you.

Lights up. Boys at the lockers watch two or three groups of students pass, offering their comments to each other, joking, and cajoling. Some team members cross – "congratulations, way to go, good game," etc.

RICK: I don't want to talk about it.

BOY #1: I told you nothing happened. Romeo struck out. Didn't even get to first base.

RICK: Shut up. What would you know about girls anyway? You haven't dated a girl since your mother potty trained you. She did potty train you, didn't she?

The boys laugh.

BOY #1: You're just sore because Melissa gave you the cold shoulder. You didn't even kiss her, did you?

RICK: I never kiss and tell.

BOY #2: Well, you'll never tell then, 'cause you ain't kissed nobody.

BOY #3: Rick, you've let us down. We looked up to you.

BOY #4: Yeah. We even voted for you for Student President.

BOY #1: Some President. Can't even make it with the girls.

RICK: You guys don't get it. I don't brag about…

BOY #3: About what, Rick? You're not going to tell us something actually happened Friday night?

There is a pause. All the boys look at RICK as he raises his head. Then he drops his chin slowly and proceeds to nod an affirmative to their question.

BOY #4: What? You mean you ….

BOY #2: You and Melissa ….

BOY #1: You guys held hands. Right?

RICK: Better than that. Much better.

BOYS #2, #3 and #4: (*together*) Ooohoo!

BOY #1: So you kissed her. Big deal!

RICK: Actually, she was the one doing the kissing. But that's not all.

BOY #1: Cut the crap. Did you get lucky, or what?

RICK: Melissa was all over me and then some.

BOY #2: Ha. Ha. You devil!

BOY #3: I knew it.

BOY #4: Yessss!

RICK: Yes sir. All the way. A home run.

DAVID *walks into scene.*

BOY #1: I don't believe you.

RICK: (*noticing* DAVID) I've got a witness.

BOY #2: Who?

RICK: David. Come here.

DAVID: What d'ya want, Rick?

RICK: Tell these guys who I was with Friday night.

DAVID: What are you talking about?

RICK: These guys won't believe I was with Melissa. Tell them I was.

DAVID: You were. Okay. Is that what you want to hear? I've got to go. (*He quickly turns and exits*)

BOY #1: No way! You stud! (*high five*)

BOY #3: Romeo rules!

BOY #4: All hail Romeo!

RICK: More later, guys. I've gotta catch up with the coach about practice tonight.

BOY #3: See ya, Rick.

BOY #2: Later.

BOY #1: Romeo. Romeo. Romeo. (*crescendo*)

A bit later MELISSA *enters and proceeds to her locker. The group of boys are talking and stop as she walks in.*

BOY #1: Hey Melissa! We heard you really enjoyed the dance Friday night.

BOY #2: Yeah. Rick highly recommends you as a date.

BOY #3: So, we were wondering, if you weren't busy Friday night, if you'd like to, you know, party with us.

BOY #4: I'm sure we'd have a lot of fun.

BOY #2: We could meet at my place. Our house has a large lawn. Big enough for all of us.

MELISSA, *without saying a word, runs to the girls' bathroom while the boys laugh and enjoy their wit. Lights up, inside the bathroom where a group of girls from the dance are talking about* MELISSA, *the dance, and* RICK.

GIRL #1: And did you hear about Melissa and Rick?

GIRL #2: What about them?

GIRL #4: Yeah, well, it's no wonder the way they were dancing together Friday night.

GIRL #3: And did you see what she was wearing?

GIRL #2: What are you guys talking about?

GIRL #4: Didn't you hear? Well, according to Donnie and Chris, Rick has been bragging about Melissa's eagerness to do Biology experiments during the dance Friday night.

GIRL #2: You don't mean ....

GIRL #3: You got it. Melissa and Rick did it.

GIRL #2: No!

GIRLS #3, #4 and #1: (*together*) Yes!

GIRL #1: And the best part is, I heard they did it on the front lawn of the school.

GIRL #3: How romantic! Romeo Rick and fair maiden Melissa right in front of Castle Rock High. (*or your high school*)

The girls are giggling and laughing when they notice MELISSA *listening in the doorway. There is a pause.* MELISSA *wheels around, exits, and runs into* DAVID *who happens to be passing by. The collision spreads her books across the hallway.*

DAVID: Melissa? Let me help you with your books. (*He picks up books and puts them into her arms*) I didn't see you there. Sorry I ran into you ....

MELISSA *suddenly turns and runs away, forgetting her pencil case on the floor.*

DAVID: (*picking up pencil case*) Melissa?!

JENNIE *enters, coming up behind* DAVID.

JENNIE: What was that all about?

DAVID: (*startled*) Melissa ran into me or I ran into her .... We ran into each other actually, and her books went flying and I tried to help ....

JENNIE: David?

DAVID: Huh?

JENNIE: Is that her pencil case?

DAVID: Oh, yeah. She forgot it after we ....

JENNIE: She seemed really upset. Give me her pencil case. I'll give it back to her.

DAVID: (*handing it over*) Oh, sure. I better get going to class. (*He turns to leave*)

JENNIE: David?

DAVID: Yeah?

JENNIE: You didn't say anything to hurt Melissa, did you?

DAVID: (*defensive*) No! Nothing! I didn't do anything.

JENNIE: (*running off*) I better catch up to her.

DAVID: That's just it. I didn't do anything.

Lights fade.

Scene Six

THE COMFORTING: MELISSA *is in her bedroom wearing a bathrobe, having obviously just showered. There is a knock at the door.* MELISSA *is startled, and only stares at the door. There is a second knock, and* JENNIE *enters the room.*

JENNIE: Melissa, it's me. You dropped your pencil case in the hallway. David found it after you left. I told him I'd bring it to you. Melissa?

MELISSA: Huh?

JENNIE: Melissa, is something wrong? You're acting… different.

MELISSA: I'm just not feeling well.

JENNIE: Oh, like the flu or something, right?

MELISSA: Yeah, that's it.

JENNIE: Well, that's a relief 'cause the way David was acting, I thought he said or did something to upset you.

MELISSA: No! David didn't do anything.

JENNIE: Melissa, what's going on? Are you and David…. Well, I don't mean to sound jealous or anything, but are you scamming my date?

MELISSA: (*looking at* JENNIE *in shock*) No.

JENNIE: I must sound crazy. I just keep hearing your name and Rick's name and David's name buzzing around the school, something about the dance Friday, that David kissed someone, that you kissed someone, I just thought maybe…

MELISSA: Stop it. Just stop it.

JENNIE: Melissa, what's going on?

MELISSA: I didn't kiss David! Alright?

JENNIE: Okay, I believe you. You didn't kiss David. Then who did you kiss?

MELISSA *stares at her, then looks away.*

JENNIE: (*sudden recognition*) Rick! You and Rick were kissing? Is he a good kisser? I mean, you know, just between you and me. Give me all the juicy details.

MELISSA: (*angry*) I don't want to talk about it!

JENNIE: (*pause*) Melissa, what's wrong with you? Why won't you talk to me?

MELISSA: You wouldn't understand. Nobody would understand.

JENNIE: I'm supposed to be your best friend. You can talk to me about anything. Remember?

MELISSA: (*hesitating*) No. Not this.

JENNIE: Melissa, talk to me. Maybe I can help.

MELISSA: It was nothing, okay? I didn't do anything…, I couldn't do anything.

JENNIE *moves to her, puts her hand on* MELISSA*'s shoulder.* MELISSA *pulls away. There is a pause, then she speaks.*

MELISSA: At the dance… something happened… something terrible. I went outside with Rick to get some fresh air. We kissed and then… (*pause*) his hands were all over. I couldn't get them off me. I was frozen… scared… so afraid. I asked him to stop, but it was as if he didn't hear me. I pleaded with him, "No Rick, don't." He wouldn't stop… told me he knew what we both wanted. I couldn't believe it was happening. I never imagined it that way…. I just wanted to die right there. But I couldn't escape. I couldn't leave. The pain kept bringing him back and I couldn't do anything. My voice was gone, my arms wouldn't move. Everything was dream-like, some terrible nightmare.

MELISSA *begins to sob.* JENNIE *is silent, in shock, but she manages to comfort* MELISSA.

MELISSA: Why? Why did he do that? Why did I let him? I never should have kissed him. I shouldn't have gone with him into the darkness. If only I hadn't gone to the dance. Why didn't I go to the movies, like always? None of this would have happened.

JENNIE: No, Melissa. It's not your fault.

MELISSA: That's not what they're saying at school. They say I'm some two-bit ho' – an easy date.

JENNIE: You know that's just gossip.

MELISSA: Then how do you explain it? Why did this happen to me?

JENNIE: It's not your fault. You were raped. It's called date rape. (*long pause as the word "rape" hits home*) Have you told anyone yet?

MELISSA: I can't tell anybody about this. Promise me you won't tell a soul. Promise me, Jen.

JENNIE: You have to talk to people, to get some help so that....

MELISSA: I can't. I feel so dirty. I don't know what to do, where to go.

JENNIE: Melissa, you've got to talk to someone. You can't let Rick get away with this or he'll do it again to someone else. (*pause*) I'm sorry this ever happened. I'm here for you if you need me. (*They embrace in tears*) It's going to be okay, you'll see.

Lights fade.

SCENE SEVEN

INNER THOUGHTS: *Light pool comes up on* MELISSA, *centre stage.*

MELISSA: I still can't sleep right. No matter how hard I try, I can't stop thinking about it. I showered three times today; before school, after school, before bed.... I still can't wash away this dirty feeling. I know Jennie's right. I have to get some help, but I'm so ashamed. Rick seemed like such a nice guy. Everyone at school knows what happened. I can feel it. I can see it in their eyes. They never used to look at me this way. Those smiles and dirty looks. Don't they understand? If only they could feel my shame. Yesterday, someone congratulated me! Told me how lucky I was to have been with Rick. I sure don't feel lucky. Most of the time, I just feel sick about the whole thing. I know it wasn't my fault (*fade centre stage light pool*) but how come I still feel guilty....

Light pool up stage right on DAVID.

DAVID: Why didn't I stop Rick? I knew what was happening. I still can't believe that he would do something like that... to Melissa. How could I let it happen.... I just froze.... Melissa is my friend and all I did was stand there. I didn't help her. I couldn't help her. That sounds so stupid... not being able to do anything. Why didn't I help? All I had to do was.... I don't know what, but I should have done something. What a coward. What a loser. If I ever get the chance again to help, I will. I promise.

Lights out on DAVID. *Light pool up stage left on* RICK.

RICK: I wonder what Melissa's doing right now. I can't stop thinking about her, about Friday night. I don't know why she didn't come back to the dance. Probably just another one of those games they play. You know, hard to get. She probably wants me to make the next move. The old cat and mouse play. I've seen it before; like Friday night, all that talk about the stars, and leading me on like she didn't want to do it. She knew what was happening. She wanted me the way I wanted her, I could tell by the way she kissed me. Hey, if you want a girl to like you, you've got to cater to her needs, right? Melissa has always liked me. After Friday night, she's gotta like me even more. Doesn't she?

Fade lights.

Scene Eight

THE CONFRONTATION: *The school hallway.*

ANNOUNCEMENTS: This is a continuation of day two. Students in Mr. Williams's class are asked to bring extra work this afternoon. The Knights (*or your school team*) will be playing Tech. Vocational (*or other rival school*) at 4:30 today. It's noisemaker day. Come out and show your spirit. Would the following students report to the office: Jay Bennet, Amanda Foster, Corey La Buick, and Deanna Ross. Thank you.

Lights up in the school hallway. RICK's *gang of boys conceals him from* MELISSA, *who is on her way to the choir room with* JENNIE. *One of* RICK's *friends pushes* RICK *toward* MELISSA.

RICK: Hello, Melissa.

MELISSA *tries to get past him.*

RICK: Hey. I said hello.

MELISSA: Get out of my way, Rick.

BOY #1: Ooooh. I don't think she likes you anymore, Rick.

BOY #2: Yeah. Maybe she's got someone else.

RICK: (*to* MELISSA) I was only going to ask you to another dance.

MELISSA: I wouldn't go out with you for anything. Now get out of my way.

BOY #1: She really doesn't like you anymore.

BOY #2: Maybe she'd like me. Want to go out with me, Melissa?

RICK: Come on, Melissa. What's your problem? We had a good time.

MELISSA: A good time! Is that what you call it?

RICK: Yeah. We danced, remember. Like this.

RICK *grabs her to dance. A crowd starts to gather.*

MELISSA: *(pulling away)* Don't you dare touch me. Don't you come near me. *(starts to cry)*

JENNIE: *(stepping forward)* She told me all about it, Rick.

RICK: *(pause)* All about what?

JENNIE: You know what.

RICK: Well, I hope she didn't leave out any good parts.

DAVID *enters on his way to choir.*

MELISSA: *(can't hold it back any longer)* You forced me! I told you to stop and you wouldn't. I kept saying no, stop it, don't, but you just kept.... *(pause)* You raped me, Rick, and I'm going to the police.

RICK: *(pause)* Rape? Police? It's your word against mine. You have no one to support your story and that's all it is. A story. *(speaking to the growing crowd)* She gets me to have sex with her and then, wham!... she yells rape. I mean, first she wants to go outside to get some fresh air, then she wants to sit on the grass and gaze at the stars. Now she says it was rape!?!

MELISSA: I said "No!"

RICK: Every guy knows when a girl says "no," she means "yes."

MELISSA: That's crap. All this time, I thought it was my fault, that I had done something wrong, but it wasn't me. It was you. You raped me.

DAVID: She's telling the truth.

RICK: You shut up, David. This has nothing to do with you.

DAVID: I saw the whole thing....

MELISSA *reacts.*

RICK: I'm warning you.

DAVID: I stood there in the streetlight and watched.

JENNIE: David!

DAVID: I just stood there.

MELISSA: How could you? How could you do that?

DAVID: I couldn't believe it was happening. I couldn't move.

JENNIE: You couldn't believe… I can't believe. I can't believe you wouldn't help Melissa and….

DAVID: I'm sorry, Melissa. I'm sorry.

JENNIE: You're sorry. That helps a lot, David. That really….

MELISSA: (interrupting)   Will you testify?

DAVID: Testify?

MELISSA: I'm going to the police. Will you tell the police what you saw?

DAVID: (pause)   Yes.

RICK: No!

MELISSA: No? Now just what does that mean, Rick? Does it mean yes or does no mean no?

RICK: It means he doesn't have anything to tell.

MELISSA: It means you're afraid. Because you know the truth.

RICK: I don't have to listen to this. This is crap. The police aren't stupid. They'll know who's telling the truth.

MELISSA: Yes. I think they will. Come on, Jennie, let's go.

JENNIE: (turning to DAVID)   Coming?

They exit.

RICK: (to guys)   Hey guys, let's get out of here.

The four boys look at RICK, look at each other, and exit stage as a group, leaving RICK alone. He hangs his head. Blackout.

Scene Nine

THE FINALE: *Auditorium that night. Darkness. Choir begins*

"Amazing Grace." MELISSA *is at centre of choir,* JENNIE *to her side.*

CHOIR:

> Amazing grace! How sweet the sound
> That saved a wretch like me!

Lights come up full.

> I once was lost but now am found;
> Was blind, but now I see.

CHOIR *lowers their heads except for* MELISSA. *There is a general fade of all lights on stage, except for a spot on* MELISSA.

MELISSA: *(solo)*

> Thro many dangers, toils and snares,
> I have already come;
> 'Tis grace that bro't me safe thus far,
> And grace will lead me home.

Slow fade of spot to black.

END

Jacquie Johnston Lewis

Jacquie Lewis is a teacher of English and drama at Thom Collegiate in Regina, Saskatchewan where she developed the drama program beginning in 1987. She has entered a one-act play in the Saskatchewan Drama Association (SDA) Regina Regional Drama Festival every year except one since 1985. Two of these plays have gone on to represent Regina at the Provincial Drama Festival.

Ms. Lewis has also been very involved with the SDA in both board and executive capacities on a regional and provincial basis. She has been a member of the Saskatchewan Education, Arts Education Curriculum Advisory Committee since 1990, and was the major writer for the Division IV Drama Curriculum Requirements document published by Saskatchewan Education in 1993.

Dianne Warren

Dianne Warren is a playwright and fiction writer living in Regina. Her third book, a collection of short stories titled *Bad Luck Dog* (Coteau Books 1993), swept three of the four Saskatchewan Book Awards in 1993. *Serpent in the Night Sky* (Playwrights Canada Press 1992) was short-listed for the Governor-General's Award for Drama in 1992. That play and *Club Chernobyl* were produced by 25th Street Theatre in 1991 and 1992 respectively. She is at work on a new play, *The Last Journey of Captain Harte*.

Ms. Warren has developed arts education curricula for Saskatchewan Education. Through the Saskatchewan Summer School of the Arts and 25th Street Theatre's Student Mentor program, she has also instructed playwriting students. In 1994-95, she will serve as writer-in-residence at the Regina Public Library.

DRAMA FROM COTEAU BOOKS

THE FLORENCE JAMES SERIES

Eureka! is number five of the Florence James Series, named after Mrs. Florence James who was very influential in the development of professional drama in Saskatchewan. Other titles in the Florence James Series are:

The Plainsman by Ken Mitchell. Set just before and after the 1885 North West Rebellion/Resistance, this two-act play features Gabriel and Madeleine Dumont. $7.95 (pbk) ISBN 1-55050-042-2

Roundup by Barbara Sapergia. This two-act play looks at the crisis in prairie agriculture along with a lively tale of love and marriage in three generations. $7.95 (pbk) ISBN 1-55050-041-4

Saskatoon Pie by Geoffrey Ursell. Set in Regina in 1906, this two-act musical comedy deals with corruption, scandal, the CPR and women's suffrage. $7.95 (pbk) ISBN 1-55050-044-9

Talking Back by Don Kerr. Set against the colourful founding of the Co-operative Commonwealth Federation (CCF), this three-act play is an engaging mix of historical drama, humour, and song. $7.95 (pbk) ISBN 1-55050-043-0

MORE DRAMA FROM COTEAU BOOKS

Black Powder by Rex Deverell. Music and lyrics by Geoffrey Ursell. This forceful and controversial two-act play deals with the Bienfait and Estevan coal miners' strike of 1931. $5.00 (pbk) ISBN 0-919926-13-4

Studio One: Stories Made for Radio edited by Wayne Schmalz. An anthology of ten pieces written especially for radio by some of Canada's best writers including Lorna Crozier, Connie Gault, Patrick Lane, and Kim Morrissey. $9.95 (pbk) ISBN 1-55050-011-2

Superwheel by Rex Deverell. Music and lyrics by Geoffrey Ursell. A satirical, witty two-act play which loosely traces the birth of the car to its present-day use — and misuse. $5.00 (pbk) ISBN 0-919926-07-X

Ken Mitchell Country by Ken Mitchell. A selection of the well-known author's best work, including his one-act plays "Wheat City" and "Gone the Burning Sun." $6.95 (pbk) ISBN 0-919926-34-7

You may purchase or special order any of these titles from your favorite bookstore. For a complete catalogue of publications – fiction, poetry, drama, criticism, non-fiction and children's literature – please write to Coteau Books, 401-2206 Dewdney Avenue, Regina, Saskatchewan S4R 1H3 Canada.

PLAY SETS

Each of the seven one-act plays in *Eureka!* may also be purchased in sets of scripts or "play sets." Each play set includes scripts for all characters plus three additional scripts for the director, stage manager and prompter. The play sets also include amateur performance rights.

For additional information, or to purchase play sets of any of the seven plays in this anthology, please write to:

Play Sets
Coteau Books
401 - 2206 Dewdney Avenue
Regina, Saskatchewan
S4R 1H3
Canada

Telephone: (306) 777-0170
Fax: (306) 522-5152

Include the title of the play in which you are interested and the number of public performances it will have. Please note that performance rights must be applied for again if a play is to be remounted, whether or not additional play scripts are purchased.